AN EPITAPH FOR DIXIE

AN
EPITAPH
FOR
DIXIE

By Harry S. Ashmore

W·W·NORTON & COMPANY · INC · New York

For Anne

CONTENTS

AN EPITAPH FOR DIXIE

CHAPTER 1

THE PECULIAR
INSTITUTIONS

O N A SATURDAY afternoon not long ago I sat in
one of my favorite houses—a house with tall white
columns, a broad entrance hall, silk brocade and
dark paneling on its walls, and a divided staircase that
sweeps upward to a long disused ballroom.

Because of the sentiment and personal circumstances of
those who have lived there, the old house has defied the
flight to suburbia; it has hung on, frayed, shabby, echoing
with lost voices, but intact. I stop by when I can, fearing
that the next time I pass that way fate may have overtaken
it. It is a house destined to become a gentleman's club, a
boarding house, or a mortuary, if it is not razed to make
way for a supermarket.

This was a warm afternoon, with dust dancing in the
sun that slanted through tall windows. I sat in a sagging
wicker chair, looking through an arched doorway to the
great hall where the mistress of the house stood in con-

versation with Aleck, the yard boy. It was a set scene, with
the precision of ballet. Aleck, a straight black man with
the clouded eyes of great age, was negotiating a settlement
for his week's work. There was some cash involved in the
transaction, based on shaky calculations on both sides, and
a great deal of barter. Ultimately money changed hands,
and a package of food. But protocol demanded something
more and I, the only man in the house at the moment, was
brought on stage and introduced to Aleck. We bowed
slightly, not touching hands, following the choreography.

"Miss Betty," he said, "is a wonderful lady. I come up
here from the country more than forty years ago to work
for Miss Betty's folks, before she was even born. The old
Judge, he always looked after old Aleck, and Miss Betty
she's looking after old Aleck now. I'm getting down in the
back, but Miss Betty she's going to take care of me. Old
Aleck knows that."

We retired to the kitchen then, Aleck and me, and in the
ritual of Saturday afternoon I poured Aleck a drink of
whisky. I poured it, by certain instinct, in the special glass,
the jelly glass set apart from the others. This was man's
work and my presence rounded out the score; otherwise
Miss Betty would have left the bottle on the kitchen table
and Aleck would have taken a solitary drink on his way
to the back door—a permissible deviation, but not a de-
sirable one.

The scene, like the house, was beyond time. Miss Betty
spoke her lines as her mother would have done; I made
the gestures my father would have made; Aleck responded
out of a memory that spanned three generations. But only

the outline was correct; the set piece was without sub-stance.

Miss Betty's horizons were not bounded by the polite lessons of a young lady's finishing school; she had earned a degree at Vassar, followed a young husband to Oxford, and gone on to help sort out the ruins of German civiliza-tion at Nuremberg. For her this warm, still day was not one of an orderly progression of Saturdays that would see the old house standing after she had taken her place among its ghosts; she was there, the last representative of a scattered family, preparing to liquidate a tradition. And the government, not Miss Betty, would take care of Aleck in his last days; she had fulfilled her obligation by helping him qualify for his social security benefits.

Miss Betty and I, and I think Aleck too, were conscious of the anachronism. The age that had created the old house and sustained it had ended. It would survive for a while in the small towns of the South and the rural places, in the ebbing memories of old men, in a certain softness of voice and gentleness of manner; but in the cities it had ended, and it is the cities that now give the Southern region its character.

Who could be certain today, if he were dropped sud-denly at Five Points in Atlanta, that he was not in Min-neapolis? Who could be sure, watching the factories slide by a train window in the smoky valleys of the Piedmont, that he was not following the course of the Connecticut River? Who might not confuse the broad fields of the Mississippi Valley, lush with green cover crops and dotted with grazing cattle, with the prairies of Kansas?

These are the signs and symbols of the New South, coming to reluctant maturity a half century after Henry Grady proclaimed it. And as it has evolved, the New South has inevitably taken its toll of the peculiar institutions that sustained the Old. There are not enough Confederates left now to muster a squad; the mule markets have closed from Georgia to Missouri; six Southern states have cast their electoral votes for a Republican president; and the Supreme Court of the United States has struck down the legal basis for segregation of the races.

These monuments do not stand alone. They mark a continuing process, with the midpoint marked by Grady's lament that for the funeral of one of her sons Georgia could provide only a minister and a hole in the ground. When the Atlanta editor called for an economic re-birth the South had barely completed the monumental task of making a place in its feudal society for a mass of illiterate former slaves. Slowly, painfully, resistant to the prodding of its zealous conquerors, the region had created, out of circumstance and compromise, an order that met the minimum requirements for survival. Now the South's own prophets called for reunion—but the union had changed, too, and it no longer had a place for an agrarian enclave nurtured on the political and social concepts of John C. Calhoun.

Huddled behind its rampart of defensive attitudes, the South managed to retain its special identity longer than any other section of the country. But the rampart was irrevocably breached by civil war and industrial revolution. It is a footless, if fascinating exercise to speculate on what the New South might have been like had the Old won its war, or avoided it. The truth is that, despite its historic insistence that it should be, the South has never really been let alone. We have not yet reached the centennial of Appomattox, and already the region has been called upon to create a new society out of the ruins of its slave economy, and, almost without pause, begin the process of dismantling it. The march of events, as Southerners reckon time, has proceeded with almost unseemly haste.

In the half century after the Civil War the peculiar institution of slavery was reshaped into three institutions of equal peculiarity. Sharecropping was perhaps the only feasible answer for white men, who had land and no cash resources, and for freedmen, who had no land and only agricultural skills. The monolithic structure of one-party politics, which was to give the region disproportionate power in national affairs, was created not for that calculated purpose but as a device for disfranchising the Negro. The "separate but equal" doctrine came into being as a means of keeping the races apart in the schools and other places of public accommodation—serving, certainly, to nurture race prejudice, but accepted, North and South, as a means of preserving order.

These, then, were the institutions—the agrarian economy, the one-party political system, and legal segregation—that gave the region its unique character in the twilight period when it struggled with its internal problems and stubbornly rejected the concepts that prevailed in the republic of which it was a reluctant part. Around them were created the conventions that ordered the Southern society. From them stemmed the slogans that held together a solid bloc of Southern politicians: tariff for revenue only, states rights, and white supremacy. Yet the peculiar institutions were under great pressure from their inception.

As an emergency measure, sharecropping served its purpose; in the long haul it proved as economically unsound as the slavery which had preceded it, creating a landless peasantry which included whites as well as Negroes and provided no stable base for the region's social and economic structure. One-party politics kept the Negro away from the polls, but it did nothing to promote efficiency in government while it did much to improve the fortunes of the demagogues who arose to prey upon the Southern people. The system of legal segregation was marked by inherent injustices which nagged always at the Southern conscience, and in time it became the source of mounting discontent among those who were segregated.

These internal pressures were matched by great forces working from without. As the century turned, a shrinking world began to pull the South back into the mainstream of history. An era of accelerating progress in communications brought the automobile, which made the most remote farm a suburb of the city, and spread newspapers and magazines away from the rail lines. Voices, and then pictures, began coming through the air, and ideas and concepts reached Southerners direct, without first passing through the filter of their own leadership. The Southern people, who had been rooted to the land, became mobile. Two wars sent the young men of the region to far places, and created a vast industrial boom which attracted tides of out-migration toward the centers of economic opportunity. There was a significant in-migration, too, as industry began a countermove to the South to exploit the region's benign climate, untapped natural resources, and vast labor pool.

The peculiar institutions could not escape the profound impact of these physical changes. The gasoline engine which powered the automobile also made possible the new tools of mechanized agriculture, reducing the demand for hand labor which was the basis of the sharecropping system. The steady increase of industrial job opportunities began to lessen the bitter economic competition between Negroes and whites. The fabulous growth of the cities and the corresponding decline of the rural South brought a great expansion of the white-collar middle-class, deeply wounded in the pocketbook by taxes and ready to provide the Republicans a respectable base upon which to erect a second party. The unions followed the factories south, giving indigenous strength to the political Left, which opposes segregation as an article of faith. And the great redistribution of population pulled down the proportion of Negroes to whites to such a degree that the maintenance of legal segregation began to lose its practical urgency over much of the region.

These changes have been accompanied by a marked rise in the status of the Southern Negro. He still remains at the bottom of the social and economic scale, making up a large part of the region's rural and urban slum population, not yet free of the traditional role of drawer of water and hewer of wood. But his physical condition has improved markedly, and his opportunities are slowly but surely broadening. In the cities there is now emerging a Negro middle class—solid, respectable, and conservative—in the void that previously existed between the upper strata of professional workers and the mass of common laborers. If the Negro's usual job is still menial, his pay has risen in geometric progression, and his increased purchasing power has made him a positive factor in the Southern economy.

The most spectacular changes have come in the Negro's legal status, which has been completely redefined in a period of twenty years. He now enjoys, or has the support of the courts in his efforts to obtain, all the guarantees and protections of the United States constitution. And it is a significant mark of his progress that he won most of these rights for himself on the field of legal battle; in earlier campaigns for simple justice he relied upon the leadership of sympathetic Southern whites, but in the series of historic actions in which he regained the franchise and saw the limits of legal segregation progressively narrowed, he fought under his own banner and in his own right.

An age is not born without pangs; an age does not die without giving cause for grief. Southerners have mixed feelings about the vast changes of the mid-century. They like the new prosperity, which for the first time in their memory has produced the pleasant sound of loose change rattling in Southern pockets. But the more sensitive among them flinch at the crassness of the new age. Those with white skin view with varying degrees of alarm the Negro's successful assaults upon the institution of segregation, which have brought him now to the last stronghold of the public schools. Those with dark skin approach the new age with caution—and there is no sign of slackening in the tide of out-migration.

The New South, like the Old, still looks upon the accommodation of the Negro as its greatest single social problem. But the dimensions of the dilemma have changed significantly. The peculiar institutions were erected around the Negro; they set him apart, as they set the region apart, and if they inhibited him in some ways they protected him in others. Flowing from them were a set of conventions accepted by both races and providing the basis for an orderly if uneven social structure. Fundamentally, the relationship was that of master and servant. At its worst it worked great hardships and gross cruelties upon those cast in the lesser role. At its best it embodied the concept of *noblesse oblige* and carried with it the obligation of the strong to sustain the weak. And there was nothing in the institutions, or the conventions, to proscribe warm relationships between individual whites and Negroes.

I have had occasion to reflect upon this in personal terms. As a boy growing up in South Carolina, my experiences were shared with dozens of Negroes—the nurse who tended me until my legs grew long enough to carry me beyond her reach; the cook; the ice man; the grocer's delivery boy; the swarm of Negro children who lived along the dirt streets beyond the white neighborhood; the house servants and the field hands on the cotton farm where I spent the summers. My daughter, growing up in comparable social and economic circumstances in a Southern state, knows only one Negro well enough to call by name —the part-time maid who is regarded as a convenience, not a member of the family. Will she come to know other Negroes as she advances toward maturity? Probably, but not in the same informal way I came to know Mary and Carrie and Nathaniel and Dan and the others who crowd my memory as I write this. Under the Supreme Court's new dispensation it is probable that some Negroes will find their way into the public school she attends, and she is certain to count Negroes among her college classmates. But the schools have changed too; they are no longer durable institutions where a child follows his parents into the same mellowing building to sit at the feet of the same teacher; the mobility of our age has robbed the relationships of the classroom of permanence, and the social orbit no longer revolves around them. Who can remember when he last sat at table with a grammar school classmate? In the connotations of the answer, I suspect, lies the ultimate, practical solution to the immediate problem of integration in public education. But they have not yet provided an answer to the emotional crisis that besets the region.

In the private places of their minds many white Southerners would agree with Albert Dent, the Negro president of Dillard University, who has said that in retrospect they would one day look upon the Supreme Court's segregation decisions as the beginning of their own emancipation— the dawn of the day when they may at last put down the spiritual burden that comes with being on the wrong side of a moral issue. But at the moment the South faces the practical problem of creating a new social order to replace a system already eroded to the point where effective communication between the races no longer exists.

The void is not unique to the South. In the new Negro ghettoes that have mushroomed in all the great industrial centers of the nation, colored people still live apart, behind barriers of extralegal segregation. For the mass the migration of the last generation has been horizontal; only the outstanding few have begun vertical ascent in the social structure. But there is a fundamental difference. The non-South, newly confronted with large concentrations of Negroes, has found their accommodation on terms of full equality a problem, but insists that it can and will be solved; the South so far has simply refused to face it.

So, outwardly, the old tragic pattern repeats itself. In 1958, as in 1860, the region finds itself standing alone in naked defiance of the nation's declared public policy. Now, as then, the border states have fallen away to go with the Union; the roll call of states that voluntarily abandoned segregation in the wake of the 1954 Supreme Court decision has a historic ring: Delaware, Maryland, the District of Columbia, West Virginia, Kentucky, Missouri, and Oklahoma.

Briefly the Upper South wavered, but in the end its leaders bowed to the Deep South. Now Byrd of Virginia marches with Talmadge of Georgia, Fulbright of Arkansas with Eastland of Mississippi; the moderate voices are stilled and the hotspurs are in the saddle. Once again a solid political front extends from the Potomac to the Rio Grande.

But behind the front the South is far from solid. A great deal, of course, depends upon where you are. In the nature of the distribution of population, and the local political situation, a man is likely to be more excited in Louisiana than in Tennessee, in Alabama than in North Carolina. Out on the fringes the new Southern cause has generated considerable passion; in the rural places the hot-eyed orators once again holler nigger and conjure up their evil visions. But the cold atavistic wind of fear has produced more bewilderment than anger. The prevailing mood is escapist; actuality is not yet at hand, and most Southerners still hope that somehow it will go away.

This time around even those who have mounted the barricades know, and privately concede, that the cause was lost before it was launched; there is no glory here, only bitterness. The battlecry is not "On to victory" but "Not in this generation." This rearguard action has been aptly described by Ralph McGill of the *Atlanta Constitution* as guerrilla fighting among the ruins of the old segregated society; it can be brutal, and it can delay the orderly process of transition, but it cannot turn back the forces that are reshaping the Southern region in the nation's image.

The primary battlegrounds will be in the courts, the legislatures, and the Congress; and a generation of litigation is in prospect. But no people can live forever with an impasse and—sooner in the Upper South than the Deep

—the effort will be resumed to find a rational means of adjusting the attitude of the prevailing white majority, which is not yet willing to accept the Negro as an equal, to that of the colored minority, which is no longer willing to accept anything less.

The task, as I have suggested, is complicated by the breakdown of communication between the races—the drawing apart which began when the Negro rejected those social conventions that carry with them a connotation of inferiority. But bridges have been erected, and despite the alarums and excursions of the moment, they still stand and there is traffic across them. At the top level of the educational structure, in the graduate schools of most Southern universities, Negroes and whites have been studying together for almost a decade. On the political front, the emergence of the Negro as a voting citizen has given him new leverage on the machinery of government; Negroes have not yet achieved public office in significant number, but they have found their place in the private places where campaign strategy is plotted. The court decisions have served to give the moral issue of segregation a new focus, and there is great ferment in the churches. The Southern denominations, Protestant and Catholic, including those that split off from their parent bodies in the Civil War, have now taken the occasion to affirm their belief that forced racial segregation is contrary to the Christian ethic.

There are those who profess a willingness to guard the approaches to these bridges with their lives, but they are a comparatively small minority; their support among the

rank and file is passive, and it takes more than acquies-
cence to maintain a crusade. Once there were only two
American attitudes toward the Negro: the passionate conviction that he must forthwith be admitted at every level
of society as a matter of moral right, and the equally passionate conviction that survival of the white race required
that he be barred forever from social intercourse with his
masters. Today there is a third attitude: indifference. It
may be seen in the Southern generation that fought the
Second World War. Few of its members share their
fathers' deep emotional concern with the crumbling of the
peculiar institutions; if they cannot be aroused to battle
for the rights of the downtrodden blacks, neither are they
willing to pay the price of blind opposition to the Negro's
effort to gain a higher place in the social scale. The view
from the picture window of a suburban ranch house may
be no clearer than that framed by the pillars of a porticoed
veranda, but it is different—and as the older generation
surrenders the places of power this is the view that increasingly will prevail.

So it does not seem to me premature to begin the
preparation of an epitaph for Dixie. Will the New South
be a better place than the Old? Materially, almost certainly. Spiritually, perhaps. Behind the façade of harsh
words and extremist laws there is already emerging the
pattern in which the South will finally accommodate its
dwindling Negro population as it moves from second- to
first-class citizenship; it will be imperfect but reasonably
effective, and in the end it will be far easier to achieve
than the accommodation produced by trial and error in the

bloodshot aftermath of Reconstruction. But the transition can be accomplished only at the expense of the qualities that made the South distinctive, and cast it in the remarkable rôle it has played in the history of the Republic. Perhaps, a generation from now when the last shovelful of earth is patted down on the grave, we shall be able to see the vanishing age more clearly, to examine its virtues without being distracted by its faults. There will be, I think, other than sentimental reasons for mourning its passing.

CHAPTER 2

THE DEFAULT
OF LEADERSHIP

IN THE WAKE of the Supreme Court's 1954 decision in the public school cases there was a remarkable moment of quiet in the South. It was not the silence of shock. The handwriting on the wall of legal segregation had clearly emerged in the line of cases involving voting, Jim Crow, restrictive real estate covenants, and admission of Negroes to Southern graduate schools. Georgia and South Carolina had anticipated the inevitable by enacting "preparedness legislation" authorizing the closing of the public schools if they were ordered integrated.

The Deep Southern governors roared automatic outrage; but those of the Upper South held their tongues or indicated that somehow or other the law would be obeyed. Most Southern newspapers, while deploring the decision as premature, counseled calm and indicated reluctant acceptance. A good many churchmen spoke out approvingly from their pulpits, and the organized denominations formally endorsed the decision as morally correct. While no one on the white side of the color bar regarded May 17, 1954, as the day of jubilo, and the leaders of both races recognized that monumental practical problems lay ahead, there was almost a feeling of relief. For better or worse, the other shoe had finally dropped.

The South, however, was reacting in a vacuum. The prospect of integration had become a reality, but the actuality was not yet at hand. The Court had carefully granted a stay of execution. The new precedent was unequivocal: henceforth no child could be barred from any school supported by public funds solely on the ground of race. But it would be a full year before even those school districts involved in the cases in point were required to take any action. In the meantime the Court froze all pending litigation and invited further argument on ways and means of accomplishing the transition it would ultimately require.

Taken together, the initial Court decision and the implementing decrees that followed it a year later constitute a remarkable act of judicial statesmanship. Essentially negative in character, the new dispensation revised the constitutional standard for measuring equality in education, but left ample room for the existing pattern of segregation to continue until there was specific showing in court of denial of individual rights. The Court pointedly avoided setting time limits for compliance, leaving maximum flexibility to the lower courts which were inferentially encouraged to take into account the realities of

public opinion in each school district as they determined
what constituted "deliberate speed."

In effect the Court invited the South to work out its
own evolutionary program for putting the newly pronounced public policy into practice. Moreover, it granted
the time for which the Upper Southern states pleaded
in their *amicus curiae* briefs. As a practical matter every
school district had a minimum of two years after the May,
1954, decision to prepare for the transition. And the language of the decision intimated that the process might
be stretched over a period of years even after legal action
had been initiated; the test for a school district under suit
would not be the degree of integration it had achieved at
a given point, but whether it was proceeding in good faith.
The National Association for the Advancement of Colored
People could claim a famous victory in the decision which
set forth the new precedent, but it got substantially less
than half a loaf in the guide lines that were laid down
for implementation.

Briefly, it appeared that the decision had finally driven
a wedge into the Solid South. Hard-core resistance was
certain in South Carolina, Georgia, Alabama, Mississippi,
and perhaps Louisiana; but the Border States began immediately to put into effect desegregation programs that
have continued since in fairly good order. In the Upper
South, while there was virtually no action, some planning
for integration began. Educators indicated that they considered the new policy one they could live with, and they
were echoed in significant number by the politicians.

The mood did not last out the summer. Its course can be charted in Virginia, which has contributed so heavily to the Southern pantheon its diminished leaders of today still enjoy an almost mystical regard throughout the region. Governor Thomas B. Stanley's first reaction was the formal announcement that he would convene a meeting of local and state officials to "work toward a plan which shall be acceptable to our citizens and in keeping with the edict of the Court. Views of leaders of both races will be invited. . . ." Six weeks later Stanley was calling his fellow governors into session to plan resistance and announcing that he would use every means at his command to continue segregated schools. Within a year Virginia had developed the doctrine of interposition and was using the full weight of the state government not only to maintain segregation in those districts that desired it, but to prevent any degree of integration in those that appeared willing to accept it.

This is the pattern that has developed now across the whole of the region. There are variations only in degree; if Tennessee has avoided the excesses of Arkansas, which is less adamant than South Carolina, Governor Clement has nevertheless bowed to pressure from the dead-end segregationists. Under its impact, ideological lines have disappeared: governors who were elected as political liberals have embraced the doctrine of defiance along with those brought to power by the conservative faction; it has bedded together such disparate characters as Jim Folsom of Alabama and Allan Shivers of Texas. And out of the state legislatures has come as remarkable a collection of restrictive laws as the nation has seen since the days of the Know Nothings.

How did it happen? Alfred Friendly of the *Washington Post,* who has examined this political phenomenon in depth, gives considerable weight to the organizational work of the Southern political leadership:

> The state of affairs . . . did not just happen. It was planned that way, and with great skill. It was the achievement of determined, energetic, and effective men. Some were organized formally in such groups as the White Citizens Councils; others acted informally, but no less effectively, in political or community groups.
>
> The speed of their work, the completeness of their control of political bodies and agencies at all levels, their seizure of the offensive, and their deftness in framing the issue in the terms they wanted—all this bespeaks a high order of skill and technique.

I would agree that there is a degree of primitive political skill behind the resistance pattern, primarily exercised by those Deep Southern leaders who have managed to impose their will on their colleagues of the Upper South. But the pattern is more the product of default than of conscious design; the forces that brought it into being have been diminishing in the South, and in recent years wise and forceful political leaders have been able to keep them in check in times of comparable crisis. This time around no one has seriously tried.

There are still entire states in the South, and districts in all the others, where militant opposition to integration

may well be the price of political survival. But over much
of the region a man who is willing to endure the abuse
of a raucous minority discovers that a considerable majority, while still deploring the necessity, is looking for a
way out of the impasse. It is, however, a bewildered, un-
organized majority, intimidated not so much by the militant segregationists as by the smothering mores of the
Southern community. It remains impotent because it remains, for the most part, without public or private leadership.

There are, of course, men of unquestioned sincerity
among the political leaders who laid down the Southern
line and insisted that it must have universal support. They
believe passionately in the Old Southern dogma of white
supremacy, and they oppose integration as an article of
faith. To such men the cost of resistance is a matter of
no moment; segregation is worth the price, however it
may be reckoned.

But allied with them and doing their bidding are men
who are acutely conscious of the ultimate futility of dead-
end resistance, and of its lacerating effect upon the South.
Their private attitude contrasts with their public words,
but they are rarely cynical. In their moments of confidence
over the ritual glass of bourbon, they concede the bitter
taste of expediency; there is, more than anything else, a
feeling of sadness as they explain that they can't help
themselves, that they have nowhere else to go.

This is particularly true among the members of the
Southern Congressional delegations. They have been in
Washington a long time, most of them, and they see the

South in national perspective. They are permanently cast now in the wearing role of an embattled minority; they put their considerable skills to the service of the cause by dragging out committee hearings on civil rights legislation and stooping to the ignominy of the filibuster. They are, they know, buying time at the cost of their own prestige and influence. And they can nurture no illusion about the outcome. One of the elder statesmen put it this way to Friendly under a necessary cloak of anonymity: "The Union doesn't need troops in this Civil War; all it needs is strings to its dollars." And he added: "If Father Abraham had been spending as much money in the Charleston Navy Yard a hundred years ago as the Government spends now, I wonder if those South Carolinians would have fired on Fort Sumter."

Perhaps the most significant monument to the default of the Southern political leadership is the Southern Manifesto, which was exploded without warning on March 11, 1956, by 19 Senators and 81 members of the House. It is a document of angry words and little meaning; it shouts defiance and declares for law and order. It served its primary purpose as a rallying battlecry for the faltering South. But it also served to drastically reduce the slim chance of a Democratic victory in the national election then only months away.

The signatories not only undercut the political party to which all but three owed fealty, but they very nearly submerged Adlai Stevenson, the candidate most of them were backing for the Democratic nomination. In the hard-fought primary campaigns against Estes Kefauver, Stevenson had resisted tremendous pressures from non-Southern supporters who urged him to exploit the civil rights issue in a direct appeal for the critical vote of the big cities. Characteristically, Stevenson had made a forthright declaration of support for the Supreme Court decision in his Southern appearances, but before skeptical and sometimes hostile audiences in California, Oregon, and Minnesota he had declared with equal firmness against restrictions on federal aid to education or any other coercive civil rights measure, and had appealed for understanding of the South in her hour of trial. His temperate position had earned him the open criticism of top leaders of the NAACP, and had given an effective weapon to the radical forces forming behind Averell Harriman, an increasingly vocal critic of "moderation." Stevenson was branded the "Southern candidate," and in fact he was—not necessarily because of the personal enthusiasm of the Southern leadership, but because of its recognition that only his nomination could prevent a disastrous split in the Party, with the extreme Northern wing taking over the national leadership.

It is a measure of the Manifesto that it was the product of what amounted to a conspiracy. It was hammered out in weeks of negotiation on Capitol Hill; many of those who signed it were defensive, later explaining their action on the ground that they had headed off something worse by watering down the original version prepared by Senator Thurmond of South Carolina. Yet with all this maneuvering it remained a well-kept secret. The first leak appeared in *The New York Times* on the morning of March 9, 1956. That afternoon I happened to be the recipient of the first official word that reached Stevenson headquarters in Chicago. There was a touch of irony and a hint of disaster in the fact that I had to relay the text by telephone to Stevenson in Detroit a matter of minutes before he went out to share a platform with Governor Mennen Williams, perhaps the most vociferous advocate of extreme civil rights legislation in the Democratic Party. The "Southern candidate's" statesmanship had been rewarded by an act of Southern sabotage.

Stevenson's bid for the nomination survived the Manifesto, but its adverse effect on the 1956 Democratic presidential campaign was profound. No one could say that any single factor was responsible for so resounding a defeat, but certainly the defection of Negro voters, North and South, was of primary importance—not only in the 1956 election, but in terms of the Party's future. This last of the true voting blocs had been built firmly into the base of the Democratic structure through the Roosevelt and Truman years, and it held firm in the first Stevenson campaign. If it has in fact become the property of the Republicans, the shape of the political future has been significantly altered.

One could argue logically with the Negro leaders that a split in the ranks would disarm the Southern moderates and leave the Negroes in that disturbed region at the mercy of the extremists. But logic foundered on emotion there, just as it did in later appeals to the Southern leaders for compromise on the platform and the ticket. The Manifesto was a final disillusionment for Negro Democrats everywhere. They had been able to make a distinction between the moderates and the extremists of the South;

they could recall 1948 when the majority of the Southern leaders refused to follow Strom Thurmond under the Dixiecrat banner; they could disassociate men like Fulbright, Hill, and Sparkman from Eastland, Talmadge, and Ellender. Now, so far as they could see, they all stood together—and where they stood, they insisted, no Negro could stand. Nor was the sharp reaction confined solely to colored voters; it carried over to a substantial number of non-Southern white voters who use racial attitudes as a sort of litmus test of liberalism, and it caused understandable alarm among those big city Democratic leaders who calculate their local political fortunes in terms of bloc votes.

It is true that the loss of a single presidential campaign was a matter of little immediate moment to many Southern Democrats, particularly since their party managed to retain control of Congress and salvage their cherished committee chairmanships. But in the long haul every signatory of the Manifesto will have to reckon its cost in personal, practical terms.

Among those who reluctantly went along were members of the first generation of Southern politicians since the Civil War to break through the political limits of their regional background. In the House and Senate they had achieved national stature; now they again bore the parochial brand which cuts them off from the prospect of one day finding a place on a presidential ticket or in a Democratic cabinet. The importance of this consideration was indicated by the fact that the framers of the Manifesto made a special dispensation for the majority leader of the

Senate and the speaker of the House; it was carefully explained in the release to the press that the two Texans, Johnson and Rayburn, had not been asked to sign because of their positions of congressional leadership for the entire party. Of obvious necessity, Estes Kefauver, then vigorously campaigning for the presidential nomination, took a similar dispensation on his own, thus permitting his Tennessee colleague, Albert Gore, to follow suit and become an active contender for the vice-presidency.

Nor was this all. If the Southerners have no vested interest in maintaining the national unity of the Democratic Party they have a deep concern with keeping it intact at home. This was why the cooler heads fought the Dixiecrats in 1948, and effectively discouraged the Deep Southern effort to organize a similar bolt in 1956. But the old one-party bastion is no longer immune to the effects of two successive Republican presidential victories. The vast surge of popular votes for President Eisenhower, which carried six Southern states into the Republican column, has left a permanent mark. And not the least significant aspect of the last election was that in some Southern states the margin of Republican victory was accounted for by the major shift in Negro votes. Only the more frenetic members of the White Citizens Councils believe that the rising tide of Negro votes in the South can be turned back or long checked; and minorities have long memories. Over most of the region the Negro vote is a potential balance of power; in combination with the labor vote it has already outweighed the dwindling branchhead support in some state elections. Thus the Southern politician has come to the day when he must count the votes a racist gesture may gain or hold for him against those he may lose. It is a nervous feeling.

Indeed, one of the great contemporary ironies is that Virginia was prompted, in part at least, to initiate the pattern of defiance by the new look in state politics. The decision finally, like all those of moment in the Commonwealth, was made by Harry Flood Byrd. Coming now to the close of his long career as the nation's most genteel political boss, the senator finds his formidable machine threatened by Democratic insurgents on one flank, and on the other by an increasingly potent Republican organization which has seized three congressional seats. An issue was needed to set the woods on fire, and a whip was needed to close the Democratic ranks; the old black magic of segregation has temporarily served both purposes.

In many ways Harry Byrd is a tragic symbol of the crisis-ridden South. If he has ruled his people peremptorily, and with an overly tight fist, he has ruled them well. His stewardship as governor was a period of necessary reforms, and no breath of scandal has touched the long line of his hand-picked successors. In national affairs as well he has emerged as the very model of a righteous conservative. Yet comes now Harry Byrd, the apostle of order, intoning the fateful words: "We have the right to resist. . . ." Does this fine Virginia gentleman here invoke the right of revolution as defined by Jefferson? Perhaps; but if any ghostly trumpets sound in Harry Byrd's ears they cannot obliterate the sound of petty bickering at Richmond—or the unseemly spectacle of his man Stanley refusing to greet the Lord Chief Justice of Great Britain at the College of William and Mary because the Chief Justice of the United States was also an honored guest.

The tune Harry Byrd called in Virginia has now had its inevitable consequence at the other end of the old Confederate spectrum in Arkansas, a state that seceded from the union with some reluctance and at one point came close to seceding from the Confederacy when Jefferson Davis in effect declared the territory west of the Mississippi expendable and ordered the bulk of Arkansas's defending troops across the river to divert the Yankees from more important objectives.

Little Rock, by any definition, was perhaps the most unlikely site in the South for a second Fort Sumter. And Orval E. Faubus was certainly the most unlikely candidate for the distinction of being the Southern governor who would attempt to recreate the sounds of the past in the very season when the first earth satellite was circling the autumn skies emitting the unnerving sounds of the future.

Still, for the time being at least, Orval Faubus enjoyed a considerable local success. Employing the familiar tools of the demagogue with a certain crude skill, he managed to blur the real issues in the Little Rock impasse—including the salient fact that when he called out his militia to seize Central High School before it even opened he was defying not only the federal courts but the local elected School Board, which over three years had patiently worked out a gradual, limited plan of integration and had every reason to believe it could be put into effect with no more than minor incident. As a result the governor's constituents, seizing upon his covert assurances that they would not after all be called upon to perform a constitutional duty some of them considered painful, and most considered distasteful, rallied to his standard in impressive numbers. In the Deep South, a cheering section led by Governor Marvin Griffin of Georgia showered the governor with telegraphed congratulations and stern injunctions to fight to the last drop of Arkansas's blood. This would have been heady stuff for any politician, and it appeared to overpower Orval Faubus—a man only recently graduated from the Madison County Courthouse, where there has never been a crisis that could not be resolved by a political deal.

In publicly appraising his own situation, the governor ranged over a good deal of recorded history. On the day a federal judge ordered him to cease and desist from using the Arkansas National Guard to prevent nine Negro students from joining some 2,000 whites at Central High School, Faubus, within careful earshot of a sycophantic reporter, gazed out a bay window of the Governor's Mansion and intoned: "Comes now the crucifixion!" On another occasion, returning from the gilded precincts of Sea Island, Georgia, to discover that President Eisenhower had federalized his National Guard troops while he was somewhere in the air over Alabama, he indicated that his reaction was identical to that of Arkansas's highest-ranking native son, Douglas MacArthur, upon receipt of the intelligence that Harry Truman had relieved him of his Pacific Command.

But on the Day of the Sputnik, in a private audience

with a representative of the *New York Times,* Orval Faubus made perhaps the most alarming comparison of all. He faced, he said, the same fateful decision that confronted Robert E. Lee when he was forced to choose between Virginia and the Union.

These utterances made some resounding, nostalgic headlines in Southern newspapers; but all they really proved was that Orval Faubus, who is largely a self-taught man, had had an inadequate teacher. The gap between Faubus' dilemma and that of General Lee was at least equal to that between the Minie ball and the intercontinental ballistic missile. R. E. Lee was a man of conscience who in 1860 reluctantly shouldered a moral burden he would carry to his grave. O. E. Faubus was a practical politician who in 1957 had managed to paint himself into a corner.

Perhaps the most charitable thing that could be said of the Arkansas governor was that he had misunderstood the past, miscalculated the present, and ignored the future. It was quite possible that his bizarre actions had insured him a third term in the statehouse; the odds, however, were at least even that what he would finally achieve was the election of an extreme segregationist in his state—who might not be Orval Faubus. The governor, as a matter of fact, on the record which in the early days he consistently pointed up for out-of-town audiences, was not a segregationist at all, and, as a result, was viewed with a cold and suspicious eye by the real leaders of the mob that belatedly rallied to provide a touch of the violence he piously insisted he had endeavored to prevent.

It may have been that Orval Faubus acted out of an odd

sort of innocence. He grew up in an upcountry Arkansas county which contains no Negroes; on his father's testimony he never laid eyes on a black man until he had turned 18 and gone off to Missouri to pick strawberries. He knew, of course, as any Southern governor must, that there was a great depth of feeling against integration of the public schools of his state. But he had, only the year before, handily survived a campaign against a free-swinging, all-out segregationist who had accused him of the sin of moderation; the governor had polished off the Citizens Council candidate by a vote of 180,760 to 83,856. As it turned out, however, the real lesson of that campaign eluded the victor—that, while a majority of the white people of Arkansas didn't take kindly to school integration, most of them were willing to make a token gesture of compliance rather than invite the certain retribution of the United States government.

Indeed, the remarkable truth seems to be that when Orval Faubus sold out the moderates who had elected him and threw in with the Citizens Councils, embarking upon the very course his late, defeated opponent had advocated, he honestly believed that he could make a deal with President Eisenhower and simply put off the dread day until after his next gubernatorial campaign. The evidence indicates that he carried this illusion with him to Newport for his historic peace conference, and brought it home intact after Mr. Eisenhower downed his irritation at being called off the golf course and turned on his best conciliatory smile.

It is not even certain that the landing of a detachment

of the 101st Airborne Infantry at Central High School in Little Rock disabused Orval Faubus of the notion that he had won, or in time would win, a great victory. In any event, at that juncture his private opinion was no longer of moment. He had associated himself with a militant minority group which insisted that the South would read out of the white race any man who bowed the neck or bent the knee to federal force; if the governor had accepted any of the compromises offered by the numerous honest brokers who beat paths between his mansion and the White House he would have promptly lost the support of his new following. Thus, in the political terms in which he has always dealt, he no longer had any freedom of action; he was back where he had started—committed to keeping nine Negro children out of Little Rock Central High School by whatever means came to hand.

And, of course, on the other side Mr. Eisenhower enjoyed no greater latitude, no matter what his personal disposition may have been in those early days when he received the dispatches from Little Rock at a country club which, as Bob Considine observed, does not admit Negroes, Jews, Catholics, or poor Protestants. All moral considerations aside, the President could no more have tolerated the nullification of a federal court order by state force than George Washington could have stood idly by in 1794 when the burghers of Pennsylvania refused to pay their whiskey taxes. Moreover, Mr. Eisenhower labored under the great weight of world opinion, which counted Little Rock as a Soviet victory of at least the magnitude of the Sputnik. And finally, however reluctant he may have been to assume the burden, Mr. Eisenhower was the head of a political party which couldn't compromise on civil rights and win the next election.

Neither, ironically, could Mr. Faubus' own Democratic Party. And so, as was not yet apparent to the boys at the Southern branch heads (but was painfully clear to citizens of the great world like Richard B. Russell and Lyndon B. Johnson), the end result of Orval Faubus' manufactured crisis at Little Rock might well be not to stay integration, but to speed it. The Southern senators who tiptoed through the civil rights crisis in the 1957 session of Congress would go back to Washington in 1958 wearing lead shoes stamped Made in Arkansas. The Republicans and Northern Democrats who had been willing to trade with them had been disarmed—and back home in New York, Michigan, Illinois, Minnesota, and California their constituents had not only applauded the presence of federal bayonets in Little Rock, but suggested that since they were on hand they might well be used to draw another dram or two of rebel blood. After Little Rock, the nation moved closer to enactment of a genuine force bill than it had been since the Reconstruction.

The South has always contended that given time it could work out its own problems; offered time by the Supreme Court the Southern leaders for the most part have so far refused to use it to make even a tentative start toward the accommodation all of them recognize must ultimately come. The South has always insisted that it was misunderstood; offered the nation's sympathy, the political leadership has spurned it and invited the nation's retribution. A

measure of the high price of intransigence may be seen
in the progression of the Gallup Poll, which showed that in
1954 only 54 per cent of non-Southerners approved the
Supreme Court decision without reservation; the figure
was 56 per cent in 1955, 57 per cent in 1956, 63 per cent in
1957. And after Orval Faubus blundered into a final show-
down at Little Rock, Gallup found that only 16 per cent
of the people of the non-South believed President Eisenhower was wrong in sending federal troops into Arkansas
—and, remarkably enough, only 53 per cent in the South
itself held that view.

Marshall Fishwick of Washington and Lee has sounded
a historian's warning:

> We can admire their courage, and (knowing how many er-
> rors we make) forgive their faults, but what can we say of
> their inflexibility? How can people who know and intuit so
> much not know that a constant posture of looking backwards
> is the hallmark of stagnation? Very few of us who purport to
> be historians know much about history. But everything we
> do know indicates that history is incapable of running back-
> wards.

It would seem that those who resolutely turn away from
the future would at least be able to read the first lesson of
the South's past: When responsible men default, irrespon-
sible men take power. This is the ultimate price the
Southern leaders, and the Southern people, may yet have
to pay before the stiff necks bend and defiance gives way
to the inevitable compromise.

CHAPTER 3

THE MINDS AND
HEARTS OF MEN

THE *mystique* which activates some of the South's leaders, and paralyzes the rest, has usually frustrated and often angered those who have attempted to analyze the Southern mind. Simple race prejudice is only part of it, and perhaps a minor part—more its product than its root. Pride is involved, and the surprisingly durable memories of a lost war. The aristocratic tradition, grossly corrupted but never finally abandoned, is a major element in the compound. And it is sustained by the Southerner's remarkable capacity for unreality, which still enables him to hold out against the logic of argument and of events.

From the beginning of the nineteenth century, Southern attitudes have been shaped by the existence of two minorities—Negroes, the essentially negative force around which the peculiar institutions were erected; and Southern whites, removed from the main stream of national life in part by circumstance and in part by choice. Although Southerners are constantly reminded of their minority status by the march of political events, they rarely accept it in personal terms, and the matter is not much discussed. Even when they concede that they are outnumbered, they nevertheless remain convinced that they are right. This is an attitude perhaps necessary to the maintenance of self-respect, but Southerners take it still further. As W. J. Cash noted in his profound *The Mind of the South,* it is an easy progression to the conclusion that Southerners in fact are the elect of God; if they are misunderstood and sometimes persecuted, so were the children of Israel.

If this notion is diminishing with the passing of time, as I believe it is, it retains enough vitality to wrap a sort of protective cocoon around the Southern young in their formative years. They are still taught their region's tragic history as though it had happened to a separate country. There is an element of chauvinism in the education of all American children, since it is designed to send them forth from the groves convinced that their nation is the greatest by both moral and material test. But Southern children have an additional comparison to make; they must measure their country against their nation, and it is entirely natural that the place of their intimate associations comes first. The nation exacts certain obligations, but it is an impersonal concept; loyalty is reserved for the South.

The cocoon, however, shatters earlier now than it used to, and lets in a chilling wind. Few Southerners progress far past puberty these days without making the shocking personal discovery that, beyond its own sealed province, their breed is not universally admired. I recall, on one of my own early forays outside the region, looking for the first time upon the naked face of contempt. It was at a gathering of newspaper people in a Greenwich Village apartment, and as the applejack blossomed I found myself in conversation with a bespectacled editor who had followed the great circle route through newsrooms from California to New York. "I hope you won't take this personally," he began, "but as it happens I hate Southerners." There followed a diatribe laced with references to a stint he had served in Atlanta, where he had felt himself an alien although his Scotch-Irish blood ran as pure as mine and had pumped through American veins as long. It was not only the Southern treatment of Nergoes that outraged him. His complaint was formless and passionate, more than anything else a sort of reverse counterpart of the Southern *mystique*. The South's very existence offended him, and to it he attributed most of his country's ills.

I have heard this, in considerable variety, many times since. Sometimes the conversation is patronizing, pursued under the guise of honest effort to understand how a man of apparently normal intelligence could by free choice live in depraved Dixie. Sometimes it purports to be admiring, based on the assumption that any literate Southerner who hasn't boarded the underground railroad must be a practicing martyr. In political circles it carries a sharp edge of aggravation reflecting the demonstrable fact that simply by its being the South has often had an adverse effect upon the fortunes of Republicans and Democrats alike. But however it is cast, no doubt is left that the South lies under moral indictment as certainly as it did in the days of the Abolitionists.

This realization is peculiarly lacerating to the Southern spirit, which is usually genial and gregarious. Southerners don't mind being different—indeed many of them tend to work at it—but like all human animals they want to be loved. Their response to the discovery that in many quarters they arouse no higher emotion than pity takes many forms. The more primitive act on the principle that a good offense is the best defense and denounce their detractors as mongrels tainted by foreign influence. The more civilized resort to charm, with which they are normally endowed by training and temperament; a polite man of easy manner enjoys a certain immunity to insult. Humor has always been a great defensive weapon of the South's public men; a skillful raconteur can convert the most bitter conversation into an amiable joke—and raise doubts that a gentleman so mellow and full of human juices could actually be guilty of high crimes. But most Southerners simply retreat into unreality. It isn't so, they say (and with their hearts if not their minds, believe); or, increasingly nowadays, even if it is so, you're another one.

It is defensiveness, then, that sustains the outward forms of the Southern mythology. But, increasingly, truth intrudes. Southerners are almost plaintive these days as they proclaim one of the necessary articles of the faith—that they, and they alone, really understand the Negro. The Negro they understood, if they ever really did, is no longer in sight; he was old Cuffey, singing in the cotton fields, grinning on the streets of the little towns, childlike and happy, inefficient but faithful, content in his place. Cuffey's son is seen across a great void. He is a somewhat sullen man astride a tractor, planning to take out for Detroit if he doesn't get more money. He is a dark skinned man in a lawyer's blue suit standing before the bar of a Southern court demanding his people's rights. He is a preacher, praising the Lord and the NAACP as he organizes a bus boycott. He is a voter impassively hearing out his old political leader with his mind already made up to mark his ballot for a Republican. And he is an ominously quiet man with a switchblade knife standing squarely in the middle of an empty sidewalk. Southerners do not understand Cuffey's son, and because they don't they sometimes feel fear in their bowels, and the twin passion, hatred.

It is not in fact a new feeling, although many Southerners have succeeded over long periods in muffling it in illusion. When John C. Calhoun declared that slavery was not a necessary evil, as many Southerners had regarded it, but a positive good, certain necessary premises were established. The first was that the Negro is inherently inferior and would be content with, or at least incapable of effectively protesting, a position that would confine him forever to the mudsill upon which Calhoun foresaw a great civilization flourishing. But to make certain that this was so, the South had not only to clamp feudal restraints on the slaves, but to protect them against the unsettling influence of education. Internal agitation against the peculiar institution—and there had been a great deal of it in the South before 1830—had to be silenced; this was accomplished by a form of social sanction that prevails

to this day. Outside agitation among the Abolitionists of the North could not be halted; but its practical effect could be turned back at the Mason-and-Dixon Line, and was until the fateful day when blue-coated soldiers marched across the Potomac.

But even with all this, with the South ordering its affairs on its own terms, there was always a needling suspicion that the iron social structure might not be entirely secure at its base. There were, as the planters began to discover, built-in agitators among the slaves themselves, hulking men who could not be finally broken to the plough and the hoe. They could be, and were, quickly sold down the river; but then there would be another black man looking out of the corners of his eyes, thinking. Although slave resistance was for the most part individual, the possibility of organized rebellion was always there. And when Denmark Vesey led his ill-starred revolt in Charleston in 1822, a cold wind blew across the lonely fiefs where a handful of whites lived among an army of blacks. No one would ever be sure again what was going on behind those dark and placid faces.

There are those who believe that this circumstance alone would have eliminated slavery in time, or drastically altered its form. No human being has ever willingly accepted bondage as a permanent condition. Those who resorted to naked force to preserve the system created active resentment, and steadily pushed the slave toward the point where he had nothing to lose by fighting back. Those who tried the humane approach obtained temporary loyalty in return, but they were embarked on a course that would inevitably raise the Negro's standards and fan his desire for freedom. Frederick Law Olmsted, touring the Cotton Kingdom a few years before the Civil War, found "no part of the South where the slave population is felt to be quite safe from a contagion of insurrectionary excitement." The question, however, is moot. There was no time for evolution. The slave system was summarily terminated at Appomattox—and no one, North or South, had given much serious thought to what would replace it.

It turned out to be chaos. Sentimental men far removed from the scene had not only declared the Negro free but had endowed him with the full rights of citizenship—and had sent down an army to see that he exercised them. The horrors of Reconstruction, like everything else Southern, have been exaggerated; but they were nevertheless real. The mere sight of black men, drunk with new-found power and carpetbag whisky, careering through the streets and clumsily pawing the machinery of government, fed the white South's ancient fear. The resort, inevitably, was to force; the old Confederates pulled on red shirts and pillow cases and took to horse to put the Negro in his place—not his old place in the slave pen, but a new place beyond the pale of white society. And, typically, they sealed the new order with a political deal; in 1876 the Confederates traded off the votes required to steal the presidency from Mr. Tilden, and in return the Republicans went along with withdrawal of the Federal occupation forces.

But there was a condition attached to the deal, and for some 20 years it was more or less faithfully observed. The

Confederates agreed to see to it that the Negro retained his essential civil rights—the vote, the right to sit on juries, and the right to hold public office. Moreover, while the social lines were drawn as firmly as ever, the Southern leaders made no immediate move to end the Negro's free passage in places of public accommodation. Former Abolitionists who feared the worst were pleasantly surprised when they came South to see for themselves what had happened after the occupation forces were withdrawn. In Columbia, Charleston, and other Southern cities they found Negroes and whites cheerfully riding side by side on public conveyances, and there were restaurants, saloons and ice cream parlors that drew no color line.

So for more than two decades Negroes continued to vote, under Southern auspices, and to hold minor office in substantial number. When the free-swinging Populists first arose to challenge the conservative Democrats they attempted to found their party on a coalition of Negroes and poor whites. And the Bourbons responded by wooing the colored vote with equal fervor. The Negro was more a pawn than a participant in this struggle for power, and its excesses led to vote frauds of such magnitude that they were used to bolster the argument for disfranchisement. There was, as one contemporary observer noted, a wonderful irony in the fact that the white South took the vote away from the Negro because there apparently was no way to keep the white politicians from stealing it. Once deprived of his political power the Negro had no way to defend himself against the advocates of Jim Crow—and there was no practical reason why white politicians should stand up for his rights. In 1896 the *Plessy* decision by the United States Supreme Court formally recognized legal segregation as the law of the land.

There followed the only relatively quiet time the South has known. It was, it is true, the quiet of stagnation. Poverty lay across the region and whites and blacks alike were occupied with elementary problems of survival. They had come, in Cash's telling phrase, to the new frontier the Yankee made. This was the time when the South stamped out the brief flare of Populist rebellion and forged its monolithic political unity, polished up its legends of vanished glory, and hammered into place the rigid bounds of social custom—including Jim Crow in all its legal and extralegal forms. Great forces of change were gathering, but they were still beneath the placid surface. Order had been achieved at last; everything was in its place, and every man, and there was an illusion of permanence about it all.

But even in the quiet time the ancient fears persisted without overt cause. Negroes were not actively contesting for a higher place in the social order. Despite the notable exceptions, they had on the whole behaved responsibly during the war and its aftermath, and now they accepted the new dispensation of second-class citizenship with remarkable grace; Booker T. Washington held up his spread fingers and proclaimed that whites and blacks could move forward separately in all things social. There were no agitators abroad in the land; the North was too busy with its booming commercial affairs to bother with nonsense like social reform in a conquered province rapidly being left behind in the great rush of westward migration. The peculiar institutions had never been so free of pressure, and would never be again—yet somehow the South found it necessary, as C. Vann Woodward has documented in *The Strange Career of Jim Crow,* to push the forms of segregation beyond anything that had been known or contemplated in the darkest hours of Reconstruction. It was not enough to physically separate the races at every possible point of public contact; it had to be done in such a way that the Negro would be constantly reminded of his inferiority.

Why? I doubt that there is a single answer, but there is a clue in the bombastic Southern literature of the period. It reflects a growing obsession with the sanctity of white Southern womanhood, and, by implication, a fear of "mongrelization." Miscegenation, it is true, was already underway on a grand scale in the region and proceeding at such a pace that a really black skin would soon be a rarity. Moreover, it was obvious that this wholesale cross-breeding was the direct product of the degradation that accompanied the extremes of segregation; whatever their desires might be in the matter, black women were available for the white man's taking. It was, however, a one-way traffic; the highest crime of all—beyond murder or treason—was the taking of a white woman by a Negro, and it made little difference whether it be by force or consent.

And here, I think, we come to the formless fear that lies at the heart of the Southern *mystique*—not much discussed these days except in the rude halls where the demagogues harangue the Citizens Councils, but active and festering still. Irene C. Edmonds, the Negro poet, has called it the Black Shadow—"the fear of Negro blood as a source of defilement."

The South, of course, has no patent on it. It exists in varying degree among white peoples everywhere and is particularly prevalent among those of the Anglo-Saxon and Nordic strains. Perhaps the shortest and most pointed conversation I ever had on the subject occurred in London a few years ago. It was at a cocktail party, American style, with too many people jammed beneath a lowering pall of tobacco smoke. I was in the middle of the crush, struggling to raise my glass, when a tall, thin Englishman appeared before me, shuffling crabwise through the crowd. He peered down and inquired, "You're the gentleman from Arkansas?" I agreed that I was. "It's in the South, isn't it?" Again I concurred. "Well, sir," he said, "I should just like to say to you that I shouldn't like to have my daughter marry a nigger either." And shuffled off.

The Englishman's answer to the unasked question would, I suspect, be that of the great majority of white Americans, Northerners no less than Southerners. The reasons usually advanced to support the objection to such a union cover a considerable range, and all of them might well be struck down by logic; the anthropologists find no evidence to support the myth of inherent Negro inferiority, and there are even those who contend that the white races would be strengthened by an infusion of blood from the colored peoples who now so heavily outnumber us around the globe. But the final deterrent would remain: an emotion that seems to have the force of instinct even though it is clearly an acquired characteristic.

I have no doubt that this white attitude will be tempered by the passing of time and the steady upgrading of the Negro people; but for practical purposes, time in this instance must be measured in generations. The key to today's dilemma does not lie in attempting to change the white attitude by moral persuasion, but in re-ordering our institutions to accommodate it as we set about meeting the legitimate demands of the minority group. This was what Howard Odum, the great student of the Southern region, had in mind when he wrote in anticipation of the Supreme Court's segregation rulings: "It was of the first importance that Southerners face the plain assumption that they did not appraise the Negro as the same sort of human being they themselves are." It is of no less importance than non-Southerners should candidly examine their own appraisal of the minority race.

Such an examination does not, it seems to me, lead to the conclusion that social segregation was inherently evil. Seen in perspective it can, I think, be defended as a necessary bridge in the Negro's progress from slavery to citizenship, a journey that could not conceivably have been made overnight. Nor is the theory that underlies it necessarily entitled to automatic moral condemnation. Pride of race, and the desire to maintain its integrity, are not ignoble. What was ignoble was the white South's refusal to recognize that in practice its effort to translate custom into law did not grant to the black South any perceptible degree of the human dignity it was attempting to maintain for itself.

For the Negro, segregation came to mean deprival. He

did not get his fair share of the public bounty; he was not accorded equal treatment before the law; he was not allowed to participate in the conduct of public affairs that concerned him no less than his white neighbors; he was blocked out of virtually all activities that promised economic advancement. These conditions, alien as they may be to basic American concepts of democracy, might have been tolerable as temporary measures—and doubtless were to the great mass of Negroes in their first bewildered years outside the slave quarters. The trouble was that the system became so inflexible that it could not adjust to changing conditions; it made no provision for judging Negroes on the basis of individual merit, but lumped the best with the worst. And it insured its ultimate destruction by allowing the Negro sufficient freedom of action to encourage a steady elevation of his aspirations while it stubbornly withheld the means of realizing them.

Thus the South found itself with a tenable social theory and an untenable legal practice. Only a thoroughly determined man could blind himself to the injustices of segregation. Separate but equal, the Supreme Court had said; but everywhere a Southerner looked there was clear evidence that separation meant inequality. Thus in those with any degree of sensitivity a sense of guilt was compounded with the ancient fear. James F. Byrnes, rushing to build an adequate school system for South Carolina's Negroes under the lengthening shadow of the Court upon which he once had a seat, said candidly: "To meet this situation we are forced to do now what we should have been doing for the last fifty years."

But even if the South had accepted the principle of equality with the same fervor with which it insisted upon the principle of separation, it would have soon encountered the dilemma that confronted the humane slave owners. Had the undernourished and inadequate public school system put together in the South only a half century ago extended equal opportunity to Negroes, it would have taught them the same lessons it taught the whites— and those lessons are based solidly on the equalitarian tradition. Even as it was, sitting in the little slab-sided shacks at the feet of semiliterate teachers, Negro children heard of Washington and Jefferson and Lincoln and learned that there is a hallowed document that says all men are created free and equal. Here, then, was the real source of the agitators the South was prone to blame for all its racial troubles; Walter White would obtain material assistance for the NAACP's crusade in New York, Boston, and Washington, but he had learned the lessons of protest in public schools supported by the white citizens of Georgia, and at Atlanta University, to which some of them still point with pride as an example of how well they have treated the minority race.

In the last two decades there has been at least tacit Southern recognition that an increasing number of Negroes were earning a higher place in the social order than the old system afforded. Although the Southern leadership went through the motions of protest in the line of segregation cases that preceded the public school decision, it accepted the adverse decisions with marked tolerance and even good will. So did the general public. There was no great outcry when Negroes began to vote, to enter without prejudice the graduate schools of Southern universities, and to sit where they chose on interstate transportation. Indeed, before the recent tide of bitterness swept over the region, Southerners had begun to publicly acknowledge some of the patent absurdities of a system that in the name of sanitation required separate drinking fountains for Negroes but permitted white infants to feed at the dark-skinned breast of a colored wet nurse. They could chuckle at the suggestion of Harry Golden's *Carolina Israelite* that the way to complete the transition was to adopt "vertical integration"; since nobody in the South objected to standing by a Negro, and everybody objected to sitting by one, the sensible thing to do was to remove the seats from the classrooms and let the next generation of school children study standing up.

The schools, it must be conceded, provide a special test. Children are involved, and the emotions naturally run deeper. Yet it is precisely here that the Southern *mystique* displays its besetting contradiction. Its basic assumption is that the white Southerner is by nature and training superior to the Negro, that there are inherent differences between the races. How, then, can it further be assumed that amalgamation will automatically ensue as a result of casual proximity in the classroom?

The South's own experience demonstrates that its fears are without foundation. In the days when the rural pattern was dominant, there was far greater intimacy among whites and Negroes than the region will ever know again; yet the social pattern as it involved home and family was never altered by it, or even remotely threatened. Companionship does not necessarily follow contact; it is a matter of personal choice that is, should be, and will continue to be, beyond any system of law.

The South can see, too, if it cares to look, that this has been the pattern in non-Southern school districts which have had years of experience with integration on a scale that is not, in any event, likely to follow in the South for some years after the bars are finally lowered. The District of Columbia, which a loaded Congressional Committee has attempted to use as a horrible example of the perils of integration, provides a case in point. In his sometimes bitter *Go South to Sorrow*, Carl Rowan, the able Negro journalist, described the scene at a Washington high school. He had just been told by a white student of a football game that ended with white players bearing a triumphant colored halfback off the field on their shoulders. But Rowan's practiced and in many ways disapproving eye saw a great deal more:

Still there was evidence that this "Hollywood ending" vignette did not tell the full story of desegregation at McKinley or the other public schools of Washington. There were scenes of racial commingling—ping-pong, basketball and a few informal chats—but scenes of racial clannishness were more numerous. Negroes walked and talked with Negroes, whites and Negroes ate in their own little racial groups for the most part.

How could anyone rationally expect it to be otherwise? The Southern *mystique* itself—whether one regards it with pride, wonder, or loathing—demonstrates that the barriers of the mind have never needed to be sustained by the barriers of law. Indeed, the final irony is that in the South's own terms there could be no greater insult than the contention that physical separation of the races is necessary to prevent the blue-eyed daughters of Dixie from winding up in the arms of colored lovers.

CHAPTER 4

THE OTHER SIDE
OF THE COIN

I N THAT GRIM time when the great depression underscored the habitual poverty of the South, I carried a newspaper route that passed through a sizeable Negro neighborhood in Greenville, South Carolina. One boundary of my daily round was the embankment of the Southern Railway tracks, where the Crescent Limited thundered by in remote grandeur and the long freights crawled past with a burden of the dispossessed covering the cars like roosting birds. The other was a festering creek that in occasional flood carried away that considerable portion of sewage the primitive outdoor plumbing could not, or did not, accommodate. There was no pavement here, and in truth no streets; the stilt-legged shotgun houses were set along muddy tracks that began, curved, and ended without perceptible pattern.

My youth, and the satchel of papers that slapped my thigh in the early mornings, or the route list in my hand on collection days, gave me innocent passage in this alien community. I came to be accepted as part of the natural order, and the pulsing life went on around me without the sudden dead pause that usually greeted the appearance of a pale face. I was, as I came to understand many years later, thus afforded a view denied to most whites; since it was understood that I could do its residents neither harm nor good, my presence did not disturb the community's natural rhythm.

The sights, the sounds, and the smells were certainly different from anything I had known in the prim neighborhoods across the tracks. There was music in the soft voices and the liquid laughter, and a kind of subdued anguish in the song that was sounding always somewhere. The cutting edge of poverty had left visible marks: the swollen bellies of rickety children, the scabs of pellagra, the hollow cheeks of the tubercular. Yet there was an astonishing vitality, too, in the broad-shouldered bucks swinging off in the dawn to their muscle-straining jobs, and in the heavy-lidded, earthy women who marked their passage with white-toothed approval. It showed even in the very old, the gnarled uncles and grannies who poked at the black iron washpots and tended the swarming children through the long days when the able-bodied were at work, or looking for it. Moving their tilted split-bottom chairs with the sun, sitting loose, as they said, they simply refused to die.

The community was close-knit, despite its obvious impermanence; and the spirit, of necessity, was communal. Only in extremes of weather were the openings of the

close-set shacks closed; normally one saw through from
front door to back, and the hum of conversation carried
without interruption from window to window and from
porch to sagging porch. No man owned the land he lived
on, and the coming and going of persons of all ages kept
the population in constant flux. With rare exceptions family relationships were casual. The usual conventions were
relaxed; bastardy carried no permanent stigma, nor vene-
real disease, nor a prison record. Yet there was a code
here, too. Everyone knew privation, but no one starved;
the fatback and greens were a shared necessity and the
Saturday night bottle was in the public domain. Sudden
flares of violence, the flashing of bright blades and the
stain of red blood against dark skin, were commonplace;
but the children ran without fear and were loved. Passion
was permissible, but cruelty was not; transgressors guilty
of sheer meanness were promptly cast out.

These Negroes were, surely, at the very bottom rung
of a social structure that was then in disorder everywhere
in America. By any measure they were worse off than
those who had remained on the land; the sharecropper
was in straits, too, but he still had the bounty of the fields,
the lonely pleasure of the woods, and the dignity of work.
This urban jungle subsisted on scraps from a table becoming increasingly bare; the rescue squads of the New
Deal had not yet arrived and the thin trickle of private
charity was drying up at its source.

The distance from nadir to zenith in the Negro's fortunes has never been great; but those I moved among in
Greenville must have been near the lowest point in the

curve. (I make no claim to knowing them; knowing implies acceptance on terms that were neither asked nor offered.) In their relations with each other they were, for all practical purposes, beyond not only the white man's law, but his notice. They had precious little to build on, it is true, but they had the privilege of ordering their primitive community on their own terms. Was the pattern, then, shaped by peculiar racial characteristics?

I suppose I thought so at the time, if I thought about such esoteric matters at all. But later, in this country and abroad, seeing men of different pigmentation trapped by adversity in the wake of depression and war, I began to wonder. Were these Negroes, in the fullness of liquor and Saturday night, any more prone to mayhem than my cousins who often stood off the peace officers in the mountain coves only a few miles away? Did they breed any more casually than the poor whites left behind on the abandoned tobacco roads along the Savannah—or for that matter, the fair-skinned daughters of Britain in the days when a randy American invasion force roamed the countryside under cover of blackout? Did they turn to petty thievery any quicker than the Germans or the French who were reduced to picking over the ruins of war? Was it lack of moral and physical fiber that ran up the disease rates, or the lack of proper diet and medical care? Was not the stench that hung over the community in fact the universal smell of poverty?

The issue I raise here is not whether one race is morally superior to another, but whether privation produces substantially different results when black men are subjected to it. The statistics of comparison are not much help; among Americans only the Negro has been held back by the restraints of slavery and segregation and there is no way to tell what he might have done without his special handicaps. This robs the standard arguments for white supremacy of logical validity; the racists have to reach far into the outfield of history to buttress their case. But it also vitiates the Negro leadership's insistence that given a clear field and a fair chance a black man can hold his own with a white. No one knows, because the sample is not yet large enough to provide the proof.

But what does seem to me clear is that the Negro's attitudes today are shaped wholly by his American environment. The heritage from Gambia, the Gold Coast, Guinea, and Senegal is only one of physical characteristics, and these sharply altered by the thinning of the African blood. The Negro, after all, has been in this country as long as the Anglo-Saxon, and his immigration was halted by law before the Central European's began. The importation of African slaves was banned by Congress in 1807, and the dwindling bootleg trade from the Caribbean islands was finished well before the Civil War. The old tribal culture was ruthlessly rooted out upon the Negro's arrival in the New World, and all contact with the dark continent ended.

Linguists still journey to the isolated Atlantic sea islands to look for traces of Gullah in the speech patterns there, but their finds are no more than museum pieces. For generations the talk of Southern Negroes, which has delighted the nation's humorists, has been nothing more nor less than an illiterate rendering of standard Southern speech. A case of sorts can be made for African influence on spirituals, lowland Southern folk music, and jazz; but I am not certain how much of this basic rhythm was transmuted from the jungle and how much simply reflects the steady swinging of the white man's axe, pick, and hoe. In any event, in those temples where the jazz cult gathers these days I have noticed that the side man on the drums is likely to be white, with the darker brethren getting in their best licks on the reeds and the brass.

I am not dismissing the importance of racial differences. They are real. Indeed they are urgent, since, as I have noted, they loom large in the white Southern *mystique*— and have produced its counterpart among the new Negro leadership. But it is important to understand that the separate society in which the Negro has lived took little, if anything, from the exotic culture of Africa; if he never had a chance to live up to them, the standards that were set for him were nevertheless those of the whites. He is Christian, not pagan. His language is American English, and given a chance to learn it properly he handles it as well as anyone else. He earns his living in a free enterprise economy. His dress, his diet, and his entertainment are not different in kind from those of his white neighbors. He has contributed something to the American culture, certainly, but he has taken much more. And he has had no communication with the black gods of Africa for a hundred years and more.

Periodically the dream of repatriation has bemused Americans, white and black. John C. Calhoun was one of the organizers of the American Colonization Society which founded the Republic of Liberia in 1820 as a repository for freedmen who might disturb the slave system. The Society had no more lasting success than did the megalomaniac project of Marcus Garvey, who a hundred years later formed an all-Negro organization to march back to the Gold Coast under a flag bearing a black star. The American Negro's identification with his old world exists today only as an important problem of American foreign policy, and an effective propaganda plank in the platform of the NAACP. In trouble, as we are, with the darker-skinned peoples who hold the world balance between East and West, American discrimination against colored people undoubtedly has a profound emotional impact in the great critical arc from North Africa to Red China. This, indeed, was a major point made in support of ending public school segregation in briefs filed with the Supreme Court by both the Truman and Eisenhower administrations, and it is used to good political effect now by supporters of civil rights legislation.

Some Negro intellectuals have attempted to establish a sort of mystic identification with the anticolonial revolution now racking so much of the world, equating the destiny of American Negroes with that of Orientals and Moslems. I once encountered this from a platform at a meeting in Kansas City, where a handsome, tense, light-skinned Negro plied me with a series of needling questions. I could only reply with what I believe to be the truth—that in any discussion of the American Negro's problems he would find far more common ground with

Herman Talmadge than he would with Pandit Nehru.

At that same session in Kansas City, the late Charles Johnson of Fisk University, who came as close to serving his people as an elder statesman as anyone I have known, turned the coin over when he replied with some asperity to another heckler: "You don't seem to understand what I have been about all these years. I'm not trying to abolish the Negro, I'm just trying to secure his rights."

Here, then, are the basic elements of the emerging Negro *mystique:* he naturally wants to be like the white men who dominate the society that has given him his values, but because of his color he hasn't been absorbed as were the minorities which lost their special identities with their accents. The Negro's reflexes are defensive, but like those of the white Southerners with whom he is at odds, the outward manifestations of his drive are becoming increasingly aggressive. There is, however, a vital interior difference: the white man takes perhaps undue pride in his race and his past, while the Negro tends to look upon his background with mixed emotions that include more than a touch of shame. This in itself is a consequence of adopted white values, which idealize breeding and the long continuity of family social rank.

It has always seemed to me that the Negro can, without undue strain on his philosophical bent, find solace in the special circumstances of his history. Until very recent years nothing that had happened to him since he was brought to this continent in chains could properly be called his fault. His degradation was not of his making; in a system stained with moral guilt he was the victim, and therefore absolved. And in the worst passages of his long journey he found a way of maintaining his dignity by meeting arrogance with tolerance. As William Faulkner once wrote of his symbolic Sambo, he loved children— not just his own, but anybody's children.

But for a generation now the new Negro leadership has been insisting that it is precisely these gentle virtues that have cost the Negro his proper place in American society. The fierce old brown Brahmin, W. E. B. DuBois, sounded the battlecry when he poured scorn on his people for their failure to seize the opportunities of Reconstruction:

> Their own leaders decried "politics" and preached submission. All their efforts toward manly self-assertion were distracted by defeatism and counsels of despair, backed by the powerful propaganda of a religion which taught meekness, sacrifice and humility.

Manly self-assertion is paramount in the credo of the new Negro leadership. It is enjoined as the individual contribution each Negro can make to the common cause. You don't have to take it any longer, he is told by his latter day prophets, and when the white man understands that you won't take it, all this will be over. In practice, of course, there is still a vast amount of compromise with these brave words, but at the point of contact on principle the stiff white neck now is usually matched by an unbending dark one.

In attempting to convert the separate but equal fingers of Booker T. Washington into a closed fist, the new leadership long ago made a bad word of "gradualism"—which bespoke the thesis of Southern white liberals that an evolutionary process would in due time bring the Negro justice and equality, while anything that smacked of revolution would only bring disaster. Now the same fate has overtaken "moderation," the Stevensonian phrase of the last presidential campaign which was declared counterfeit almost before it was minted. Reporting on his most recent tour of the South, Carl Rowan wrote:

The men who really disturbed me were the so-called "moderates", the new weeping Willies of the South, who seemed willing to contribute so little to progress and so much to the stagnation of the ideals of the nation. Sure it is unpopular nowadays to attack "moderation." The cliche peddlers have put it next to motherhood and patriotism. But who are these "moderates"? For what are they "moderate"? Are they moderately *for* or *against* compliance with the United States Supreme Court's decision?

Rowan answers his own questions in these bitter words:

Apparently a "moderate" is any white Southerner who can prove that he hasn't lynched any crippled old Negro grandmothers during prayer-meeting hour.

And it is noteworthy that the young Negro journalist does not limit his condemnation to the South. He is equally stern in his indictment of the Eisenhower administration for its failure to take a firm stand behind the Supreme Court, and he finally describes his equation of moderation with cowardice as "a national sickness—for which the germ-carriers are both Democrats and Republicans."

This is the traditional view of the crusader, who sees the hosts of righteousness huddled, rumps together, horns out, in a hostile world. The new Negro leadership, indeed, has progressed in a few short years to the point where it might well emblazon upon its coat of arms the slogan long ago adopted by the embattled white South: We figure a man who's not for us must be against us. This reaction by the Negro leadership is as understandable as it is inevitable; in the nature of human conflict excesses on one side beget excesses on the other. I do not, however, share the dim view of those—and so dispassionate and professional a pulse-feeler as Samuel Lubell is in their number—who fear that the new rigidity of the Negro leadership countered against the surface adamance of the white South has produced an impasse that will not be resolved this side of widespread violence. The issue will turn finally, I think, upon the question of how many Southern Negroes presently march in the great crusade, and how rapidly the ranks will swell.

There is not, I think, any longer reason to doubt that the Negro leadership bespeaks the heart of the Negro people. The pathetic Uncle Toms who still occasionally dance their feeble jig in the pages of white Southern publications are talking through their tattered wool hats when they proclaim that Negroes really prefer segregation. Every credible bit of evidence indicates that those in the South, no less than the migrants to the great cities, have long since emotionally rejected the old separate but equal concept. Indeed, it is doubtful that any man of any color or condition this side of feeble-mindedness was ever pleasured by a dispensation that clearly implied that he wasn't good enough to associate with his neighbors.

But this is still for many, and probably for most, Negroes

more a matter of emotion than of action. It does not yet imply a mass willingness to attack the peculiar institutions head-on—to run the certain risks and incur the discomfiture of any crusade against the established order. This condition is not the product of the absurd new restrictive laws or the breast-beating and overt acts of economic intimidation by the Citizens Councils. It is one of the great ironies that the reverse is true; the Southern zealots have succeeded only in rubbing up the natural resentment of Negroes who might otherwise have been disposed to avoid an active role in the new crusade. The failure of so many Negroes to rush forward at the sound of the bugle is, I believe, due to the fact that they simply are not yet equipped to exercise the rights they deeply believe should be theirs.

This inertia is the great frustration of the new leadership. The statesmen of the crusade, men like Lester Granger of the Urban League and Ralph Bunche of the United Nations, and field commanders like the late Walter White, Roy Wilkins, and Thurgood Marshall of the NAACP, enjoy the respect and even the adulation of their people. Negroes everywhere give them their hearts—but only a relatively small minority follow up with their money and their time. Voting figures provide a telling index. The outlawing of the old white primary in 1944 was hailed by the Negro leadership as perhaps the most important single advance gained in litigation—potentially even more significant than the school decisions. The NAACP confidently predicted that 3,000,000 Southern Negroes would be registered by 1956, and launched an intensive educational campaign to get them to the polls. Yet the most reliable estimate, by the Southern Regional Council, is that only 1,230,000 were actually on the rolls in the last election. The total undoubtedly has been cut by legal restrictions and extralegal intimidation in the Deep South; yet even in those states where Negroes vote freely the increase is far short of initial predictions, and the rate of gain has fallen off in recent years.

What happened, I believe, is that the upper strata of the Negro population rushed forward to qualify as soon as the voting lists were opened, and thereby quadrupled Negro registration in the region almost overnight. The remainder, which constitutes the considerable majority, simply didn't figure the privilege was worth the trouble.

This seems to me the natural consequence of a fundamental fact the Negro leadership is loath to recognize and tends to discount when it cannot be avoided. Negroes, like any other people, are conditioned by their environment— and most of them still live in a rural or urban slum. The general prosperity of recent years has reduced the degree of privation, and the worst of the jungles have given way to the bulldozers of slum clearance. But even though individual income levels and public services have improved markedly, depressed areas still exist, subjecting those who live there to the debilitating effects of inferior physical and cultural background. While, as I have noted, the general upgrading of the economy has made it possible for an increasing number of Negroes to graduate into the middle-class, for every one who has overcome the deficiencies of his origins or created an atmosphere in which his children can, five are still hemmed in by their own ignorance as well as the white man's prejudice.

Political lethargy is only one manifestation of this unpleasant truth. The Urban League, which is primarily concerned with the economic advancement of the city-dwelling Negro, has found that in the nation at large there are more skilled jobs available to Negroes than there are Negroes competent to fill them. And it shows, too, in the lack of effective Negro leadership at the community level, which stands in marked contrast to the brilliant planning and execution of the legal crusade conducted by a small disciplined group centered in the NAACP. Of the new generation in the South, only one so far stands out in the area of action—Martin Luther King of Montgomery, who rallied an entire community to his bus boycott and then achieved the even more remarkable feat of holding his followers firmly to his line of Christian passive resistance.

These, of course, are facts with which the Negro leadership ultimately must deal. Yet their concession entails an obvious tactical disadvantage, buttressing the arguments of those who point to the deficient background of most Negroes to support their contention that no Negro should be allowed to attend a white school. Here turns the old circle in which the Negro has found himself trapped in the segregated neighborhoods of Northern cities: the inadequacy of his environment confines him to second-rate educational facilities which compound the ignorance which created the environment in the first place.

This condition is now unique to Negroes and the comparatively small infusion of Puerto Ricans who have come lately to the Eastern cities. But it was not always peculiar to the colored races. The Negroes who have journeyed forth from the South in the last two generations have come by a different route to the point reached before them by earlier immigrants from the old countries of Europe. Indeed, they often have filed into existing ghettoes as they were vacated by Poles, Italians, Jews, Germans, and Irishmen moving outward into the cities and upward in the social structure. The Negro's status as a member of America's "visible minority" may make his further journey more difficult than it was for those who were set apart only by language, custom, and religion; but it will not, I am convinced, make it impossible.

A similar pattern is belatedly emerging in the South. The great waves of European immigration bypassed the region for the most part because the South had few of the expanding industries that came to depend upon the flow from abroad to meet their manpower needs. It was not, however, a direct journey from Ellis Island to the machine in a new factory; those already on the ground moved up to the skilled jobs first, and the new arrivals filled in the menial posts left vacant or created in their wake. The virtual termination of immigration early in the century created a vacuum that has been filled by the only major domestic labor surplus upon which it could draw—that in the South. Now, however, the region, moving toward an urban, industrial society at an accelerating pace, is creating a comparable vacuum of its own—sucking whites and Negroes alike off the land and into the expanding cities. Here too the latest arrivals take their initial purchase on the bottom rung and begin a journey that, if it is complicated by the deeper roots of Southern prejudice, heads inevitably in the same general direction.

In a sense this is a mass movement, and this is the character the Negro leaders seek to give it as they assail the walls of prejudice and custom. Yet this is also an individual journey for each Negro who undertakes it. Some will move faster than others, according to their natural endowment, and many of this generation will not move perceptibly at all. Robbed by their slum heritage of the heart and the skills for a fight against odds, the mass of Negroes for some years to come will not be able to grasp the new opportunities that surely will open to their race—and for them the great crusade will produce only new frustrations and mounting tensions.

This is the great unmet challenge of the new Negro leadership as it moves now into the void left by erosion of the old concept of *noblesse oblige* under which the white leadership recognized, if it did not always discharge, the obligation to look after Negroes who were denied the means of looking after themselves. It is a part of coming of age; a man who asserts his rights immediately acquires responsibilities to match. And in the difficult adjustments that lie ahead the Negro leadership can no more afford to flee from reality than can the white.

For the white leaders the reality is that the South cannot expect to stand long against the tide. Their practical problem is to bring the peculiar institutions up to date, recognizing that the arbitrary limits of segregation now deny an increasing number of Negroes the means of realizing their demonstrated potential. For the Negro leaders the reality is that rejection of gradualism as a philosophical concept does not alter its validity as a fact of life. Their practical problem is to evolve a strategy which recognizes that while a right may be defined by a court of law, it will not be secure until each individual has earned it.

It is true, of course, that neither leadership has complete freedom of action; emotional waves beat against both and I am not sure which now sustains the greater pressure. I have found as great a disparity between the public posture and the private views of Negroes as I have among whites. "Uncle Tom" is as devastating an epithet when hurled against a compromising colored man as "nigger-lover" is when applied to a white who suggests coming to terms. It is, admittedly, hard for reason to prevail in such an atmosphere; yet surely there must be those on each side who recognize that the Negro's cry of "now," and the white man's reply of "never" are a prelude to bargaining, not to battle.

Samuel Lubell has suggested that race relations in the South have deteriorated to a point where there should be a great gathering of white and Negro leaders, perhaps under presidential auspices, not for further discussion, but for a full-fledged peace conference. He may be right, but I have an idea the practical result would only be to provide another forum for grandiose proclamations by both sides. But certainly there are going to have to be many bargaining sessions on the local level—off the record, hair down, where a man declares what he wants and then finds out what he can get. The nature of our decentralized public school system will provide the occasion for this sort of negotiation as litigation proceeds under the Supreme Court's integration ruling and knocks down the preposterous road blocks of interposition. There has already been a fair amount of it in those areas where the local leadership has swallowed the principle and moved on to grapple with the fact. But, as the feeble human relations agencies of the South have discovered, no such discussion holds together long unless there is a concrete matter at hand; otherwise the session founders on the abstractions of the old moral argument in which neither side is willing to give quarter. When an order is entered, however, under the Supreme Court's original injunction that no judge shall set himself up as a school board to determine administrative matters, the issue resolves into a tangible question of how many Negroes shall go to which school and how soon— and the choice is between compromise and closing down.

How long will such a process take? Time is the elusive element in all of this; it is difficult to measure, even speculatively, because of the vast variety of Southern attitudes behind the monolithic façade. My guess would be that you would have to figure a generation at the inside in those rural areas where the Councilmen hold sway, and perhaps even in those states where the voters at the branch heads still control the political process. But I believe we will see a beginning, at least, within five years at the outside in the cities of the Upper South. And the saving factor may well turn out to be that in those areas where the white resistance is greatest, the Negro pressure for action is weakest. Perhaps the most meaningless crime of the century was the brutal murder of Emmett Till in backwoods Mississippi. The Negroes of that depressed area needed no such demonstration to remind them that as a practical matter they were virtually without rights in any direct conflict between real or fancied Negro and white interests. There ignorance lies like a pall over white and black alike, and a Negro crusader is no more likely to arouse a popular response than a white man making an appeal to reason. Yet, even while a Mississippi jury was reducing the Till case to a travesty (and thereby raising it to the historical status of John Brown's raid on Harper's Ferry) a hundred and fifty miles away at Little Rock the local school board was quietly going ahead with a plan for gradual integration that in a direct test at the polls had encountered only minority opposition—and certainly would have succeeded with no more dislocations than those encountered in Nashville and Charlotte had not Governor Faubus tossed his political monkey wrench into the works at the last moment.

There is not, I am afraid, much comfort in the shape of the future for the crusaders on either side, or much prospect of soon ending the old wearing debate. There is, however, reason to hope that the stiff necks will bend before the hard heads are knocked together.

CHAPTER 5

TO THE
MANNER BORN

IN THE ALMOST two hundred years between John
Smith's landing at Jamestown and the close of the
American Revolution, the South had its beginnings,
and virtually its being, in a thin strip of tidewater land
along the Atlantic and Gulf Coasts. In Virginia's Northern
Neck and around the new capitals of Charleston, Savannah, and New Orleans, stately mansions arose along the
estuaries, and were populated by a small but authentic
aristocracy.

It was, in form, a society transplanted from the English
countryside, although French influence left its stamp on
Louisiana and more lightly on South Carolina. The planters assumed the manners and the trappings of the British
gentry. And if they had only tenuous claims to the royal
arms of St. George and St. Andrew, they nevertheless
began to evolve a system of hereditary family rank of their
own. Although they were not prefaced by titles, even

before Yorktown names like Washington, Lee, Legare, Beauregard, Pinckney, Hampton, and Stuart bore the stamp of status.

This is the group that gave the South the legend it would live by—the durable myth that is still being worked, at good profit, by an army of historical novelists and Hollywood filmsmiths. For convenience, W. J. Cash grouped these original ruling families under the title "Virginians," and in *The Mind of the South* he made a diligent effort to determine how numerous they were, and how much they actually contributed to the opening of the interior after the cotton gin spread the plantations far beyond the lowland rice and indigo preserves. His answers were not very, and not much.

Using the test of ownership of slaves as a guide, Cash calculated that in the whole of the Old South in 1860 there were only four to five thousand of the greater planters, men with sufficient wealth to afford the pretensions of aristocracy. And of these he estimated that less than five hundred were actually of the old blood.

The reason was simple enough. By 1800 the scattered coastal communities had existed long enough to take on the patina of age and order, but the rest of the South was frontier. The men who would swarm around the base of the Appalachians in the wake of Boone and the trappers to push back the forests to the Mississippi and beyond were not pantalooned dandies. Pioneering has never been work for gentlemen; it calls for a hardier breed, on the order of the Scotch-Irish yeomen who came pouring in through the port of Philadelphia and found their first resting place on the upland slopes of the seaboard states. The parsons who carried the cross and the schoolhouse west were far more apt to be Presbyterian than Episcopalian.

Yet the Virginians were vastly important to the Old South, not so much because of what they did as because of the image they fixed in the Southern mind. The ruder men who were cutting down the trees and draining the swamps in Alabama, Mississippi, Tennessee, Arkansas, and Texas accepted the old Tidewater society as an ideal. They might work in the fields beside the blacks; but the goal of the sweating and straining in the raw new land was a big house on a hill, replete with white columns at the front and slave quarters in the rear. And a fair number of big houses did arise, some of them encompassing the log cabins in which their masters had first settled. If, in the first generation at least, they were tenanted by men not much given to reading Virgil—or anything else too difficult to be followed with a stubby finger—the forms of gentility were accepted and observed as well as they could be in a remote country from which the Indians had just decamped.

Perhaps the most objective contemporary view of the developing interior of the South was set down by Frederick Law Olmsted in *The Cotton Kingdom*. He made his leisurely journeys to the far point of plantation penetration in Texas in the years just before the Civil War, when the old slave economy had reached its full development. He found the big houses and their inhabitants no more than a thin crust overlaying a turgid frontier society that

included small farmers, poor whites only a little cut above
the bondsmen, and a significant remnant of the buck-
skinned woodsmen who had preceded the men with the
ploughs. Yet even then the duties and responsibilities of
government were largely left to a comparative handful of
ruling families who provided the lawmakers and the mag-
istrates. Those who accepted the prerogatives and dis-
charged the obligations of aristocracy obtained their rank
by circumstance, not by lineage—but then so had the
original Virginians, who most often came not from the
English manor houses they emulated, but from the debtor
prisons of London.

This important truth about the nature of the original
Southern aristocracy has been obscured by a preoccupation of later generations with genealogy so intense it has
long provided a genteel living for the spinsters of both
sexes who fashion family coats of arms. It was a society
that observed the feudal forms, divided into a small ruling
class, a substantial mass of self-sufficient yeoman farmers,
a larger group of poor whites never far removed from
that form of peasantry called sharecropping, and at the
bottom the Negro slaves whose sole function was to provide a source of menial labor. Yet the demarcation was
blurred from the outset. For one thing, family blood lines
frequently ran from the very bottom of the white social
structure to the top; the squire in the big house might very
well have a first cousin scratching the thin soil on a patch
farm down the road. For another, the frontier character
of the Southern interior made for great social mobility;
fortunes were made overnight and lost as quickly. A man

did not need a large stake to acquire vast land holdings if he were willing to keep pushing west; but he did need stamina and acumen to make the first big killing in cotton and hold on to it.

But if the personnel of the ruling class was subject to change, the economic considerations that bound it together were not. Slavery and cotton provided the mortar for a baronial society that turned out enough statesmen to keep it going for more than half a century in a philosophically hostile republic, and enough soldiers to defend it ably when the statesmen finally made their fatal error. It provided, too, one political philosopher of the first rank, John C. Calhoun, who was buried in glory in Charleston but came in fact from the Scotch-Irish stronghold of the upcountry—the icy logician who fashioned a major instrument of government in his doctrine of the concurrent majority only to see it permanently corroded by his attempt to defend slavery on moral grounds. And if, even after the inhabitants of the big houses acquired both leisure and learning, the South produced no poets of consequence, it really didn't need them. After all, it had the Cavalier romances of Sir Walter Scott who, it has been observed, probably had more to do with bringing on the Civil War than Harriet Beecher Stowe. It is hard to believe that these men of large affairs dwelt in cloud-cuckoo land, but how else explain the strange career of which Margaret Mitchell had Rhett Butler observe: They were the only race in history to launch a war when they didn't even own a cannon factory.

If the lesser orders in the Old South did not share the

grandiose delusions of the leadership, there is no evidence that they sought to alter the course of events. This despite the fact that from the beginning there was cleavage of economic interest between upcountry and low; generally speaking, the big plantations ran out with the rise of the land from the coastal plains and the river valleys, and the Piedmont country developed small, family-worked farms where slaves were few. Still beyond, where the hills became the mountains of the Appalachians and the Ozarks, there remained the last domain of the woodsmen who in fierce independence would ignore not only the slave society but the war it produced. But if the yeomen occasionally grumbled, they made no effort to seize power from the gallants who rolled their periods in the legislatures and the Congress. And when the bugles finally sounded these were the men who went down to the little villages to muster into the brigades that would follow the hotspurs under the banners of the Lost Cause.

It was one of these, certainly, who in Douglas Southall Freeman's anecdote offered the final proud and bitter summary of the war they did not desire but fought so well. He had been left on the field for dead after the last engagement before the surrender at Appomattox—tattered, starving, scarred by Minie ball and saber. But when four spruce Yankee soldiers sprang out of the underbrush to level their muskets at him and cry, "We got you!" he could still grin through his whiskers and reply: "Yes, and what a hell of a git you got!"

The war, of course, robbed the old feudal society of its substance; the slaves were set free and the credit that

sustained the cotton economy was wiped out. Yet, remarkably, the form survived—indeed, in corrupted, fragmen-
tary fashion survives to this day. When one reads the
Charleston News and Courier in this year of grace a full
appreciation of its fulminations requires the understanding that the *Courier* does not regard racial integration as a
separate evil, but as the inevitable consequence of a trend
it has been vigorously deploring for some seventy-five
years. Thomas R. Waring, the ninth-generation Charles-
tonian who sits in the editorial chair, entertains no doubt
that his predecessor and uncle, W. W. Ball, was correct
when he argued in *The State That Forgot* that South
Carolina's troubles really began when it started playing
fast and loose with the franchise and thereby let rude,
unlettered white men displace the old breed in the seats
of political power. The *Courier* naturally has no scruples
about rejecting a decision of the United States Supreme
Court or an act of Congress; it believes, as it always has,
in aristocracy, not democracy, and it has no apologies to
offer for the incident at Fort Sumter.

This unshaken faith in the aristocratic tradition seems
to have carried with it the same sense of unreality that
beset the original practitioners. Thus we find the youthful
and eloquent father of interposition, James Jackson Kilpatrick of the *Richmond News Leader,* writing a tract in
defense of states' rights which seems to assume that nothing of consequence has happened since Calhoun concluded his last debate with Webster. In *The Sovereign
States,* Kilpatrick simply contends that when the colonies
originally delegated powers to the federal union they did

not permanently surrender them, and therefore may take them back at any time. This clarion call for another try at nullification has moved William S. White, the fond biographer of the United States Senate and something of a states' rights man himself, to observe that Kilpatrick takes his constitutional theory so straight that it is 100 per cent Bourbon without a drop of branch water. White suggests that the heady potion leaves out this thinning fact:

The Civil War clearly fixed certain decisions, no matter that they were never proclaimed. One was that this country had by force of arms been made an indisputably indissoluble federal structure and that a majority would never tolerate the infinite state separatisms—and possibly the plain anarchy—that the Kilpatrick policy would inevitably bring about.

Another result of the War of no less consequence to the South was the total destruction of the means of sustaining its aristocracy. Some degree of economic security is required not only to maintain the outward forms of rank, to keep the big house painted and the silver polished; it is also essential to the spirit of *noblesse oblige*. A man who cannot meet his financial obligations is in no position to discharge his human obligations to those who have long been dependent upon him. The disposition toward charity and the humane tolerance of the foibles of lesser men—these things too have their price.

It was a price the old aristocrats could not pay in the decades of poverty that followed the war. Nor could they find their way back to their old financial eminence without abandoning the standards of honor and chivalry they had lived by, or pretended to. There was money to be made out of the wreckage, it is true; but it required a sort of scheming ruthlessness that violated every tenet of the old faith. There were two routes to wealth: a man could stay on the land and turn a profit on the depressed cotton market by sweating his white and Negro labor, or he could set up in town as a supply merchant, piling up the interest on the credit he extended in kind. Cash has written a poignant description of the Virginians as they faced the dilemma:

Some of them simply refused to compromise at all: not only would not stint and cheat their dependents, but even clung to the better part of magnanimity; managed somehow to reconcile the assiduous practice of thrift with the maintenance of the old liberal-handed spirit toward the available means; and, in a word, declined to make themselves stingy or mean or petty in any fashion whatever. They wore their patches, they carried lean jowls, they denied themselves and their families, and, if must be, they paid the penalty of economic ruin or decay (and, for all their superior energy, it was so in many a case) with high pride, unflinching and undismayed.

But these were the ones who disappeared, leaving the land behind them or letting it fall into disuse as they lived out their lives behind gates locked against reality. The others compromised—often reluctantly, as Cash said, falling back by inches, and no further than was required to avoid extinction. But in the end they joined the larger company of successful men who had had no such compunctions to put down in their rise to power. To a few of these belong the epithets carpetbagger and scalawag, but most were simply native Southerners of the lower rank who combined energy with the natural talents of the horse-trader.

What amounted to the last stand of the Virginians turned out to be their undoing. It was they who brought the industrial revolution to Dixie—not primarily to improve their own fortunes, but as a matter of public policy in a time of desperate need. By the turn of the century five-cent cotton had produced almost universal misery in the region and it was clear that the army of dispossessed poor whites would find no salvation on the land. Something had to be done to provide them the means of subsistence and Henry Grady offered the answer: take a leaf from the Yankee's book, bring the cotton mills to the cotton fields. And so they did, with an evangelical drive the pure profit motive could never sustain. Money was raised in bits and pieces, by public subscription that did not scorn so small a sum as a dollar. And when the first factories went into production, they were headed, as Gerald W. Johnson has noted with awe, not by hardheaded businessmen but by doctors, lawyers, teachers, planters, and even clergymen:

This procedure is as inexplicable as the ravings of the wildest Bedlamite until one remembers the spirit in which the whole venture was conceived, but then it becomes understandable, if not logical. This was not a business, but a social enterprise. Any profit that might accrue to the originators of the mill was but incidental; the main thing was the salvation of the decaying community, and especially the poor whites, who were in danger of being submerged altogether. The record of those days is filled with a moral fervor that is astounding. People were urged to take stock in the mills for the town's

sake, for the poor people's sake, for the South's sake, literally
for God's sake. . . .

So the mills came, spawning their ugly company towns
and pulling their hands in from the depleted farms for
miles around. From the outset they bore the imprint of the
old feudal system, both in the paternalism of the original
proprietors and in the rigorous exploitation of the cannier
men who inevitably took over the management as it became apparent that not only social service but large profits
were possible. And, although the weekly wage and the
credit at the company store offered a far better living to
most of the poor whites than the land did, it seems to be
a fact that those who came to tenant the villages were of
the weaker sort.

The company towns created a depressed, self-contained
society, subjected to long working hours from "can to
can't," irregular income during seasonal layoffs, and a
system of credit at the company store that bound the
workers to the looms just as they had been bound to the
land by the supply merchants. So the "lint heads" came
to be scorned by the more ambitious whites, who felt with
reason that to join them meant the abandonment of all
hope of personal advancement. And the mill village had
no attraction for the wild breed that populated the higher
land; it was no place for a man like old Fitz Linkhorn in
Nelson Algren's *A Walk on the Wild Side:*

"I ain't a-playin' the whore to no man," he would declare
himself, though no one had so charged him.
Six-foot-one of slack-muscled shambler, he came of a sham-
bling race. That gander-necked clan from which Calhoun and

Jackson sprang, Jesse James and Jeff Davis' people. Lincoln's people. Forest solitaries spare and swart. . . .

Whites called them "white trash" and Negroes "po' buckra." Since the first rock had risen above the moving waters there had been not a single prince in Fitzbrian's branch of the Linkhorn clan. . . . When a Linkhorn had finally taken bush parole, fleeing his Scottish bondage for the brave new world, word went on ahead: Watch for a wild boy of no particular clan, ready for anything, always armed. Prefers fighting to toil, drinking to fighting, chasing women to booze or battle: may attempt all three concurrently. . . .

Fierce, craving boys, they craved neither slaves nor]
. . . yet they had seen how the great land owner, the mor.
he got a few black hands in, put up his feet on his fine porch and let the world go hang. So the Linkhorns b
their own narrow backs against their own clapboard sh
pulled up the jug and let it go hang too. Burns was still t.
poet.

The Linkhorns didn't check into the cotton mill villages at all, and the Virginians who founded them did not last long at the roll-top desks of management—or if they stayed, they soon conformed to the pattern that made return on the investment more important than the condition of the hands. Indeed, the cotton mills were symbolic of the whole new age of Progress. With them came the Chambers of Commerce, the Rotary Clubs, the schemers and the speculators, the fixers and the hucksters, local land booms, and yellow brick churches called "plants" by their pastors. Atlanta began to look like Minneapolis.

A Virginian could survive in this new pushing social order only by detaching himself from it. The old concept, which called for a concern with abstract notions of honor at least equal to the concern for concrete matters of profit,

no longer carried automatic respect; and the old vices—
a civilized devotion to liquor, gambling, and gay ladies—
came under the rigorous condemnation of the new breed
of Protestant ministers who became apostles of Progress,
condoning child labor while they demanded that the full
police powers of the state be brought to bear on the individual sins of the flesh.

This change in the ruling class, then, was a long-running
process of mutation. It has continued until there is little
left of the old aristocracy now except the manner, which
ill generally adopted by those in the upper reaches of
power structure. I am not suggesting that there are
men in the South who will, in a time of testing, place
devotion to the common weal above their self-
erest. I am suggesting that in the South, as in the nation
at large, this is not now the mark of caste, but of ec-
centricity. The old, fierce individuality which tempered
pride with magnanimity has given way to a sort of calculating caution which measures progress solely in terms
of personal gain.

The process is best described, I think, in the volumes
that make up the great Gothic structure of William Faulkner's saga of Yoknapatawpha County. In some ways Faulkner's view is special, since Mississippi has now become
atypical of the new urban South. Yet the conflict between
the Sartorises and the Snopeses, traced over the generations and exaggerated into poetic symbolism, is central to
the story of the transition of the Old South to the New.
It was not that a Snopes could best a Sartoris in any direct
test of strength; rather it was that the Snopeses, with their
eyes fixed unwaveringly on the main chance, could outlast

the Sartorises and finally displace them in the big house on the hill. The essence of the Faulknerian tragedy, then, is the fatal weakness of the Sartorises themselves. They were capable of great dreams, and of great deeds, but always they relied more on emotion than on logic; they saw the world not as it was, but as they wanted it to be, and they built their faults as well as their virtues into the society they created and controlled. In the end it was time, not the Snopeses, that brought down the Sartorises; the Snopeses simply stood by, unbemused by notions of honor and chivalry, ready to move bit by bit into the vacuum created by the steady decline of the old order.

Sentimental Southerners may mourn the change, as Faulkner does. But practical Southerners must recognize that there will be no turning back, that when the *Charleston News & Courier* issues its call for all good men to come to the aid of the Old South, it is not a Hampton who steps forward, but one of the Snopes boys, mentally calculating the possible profit from the dues of a Citizens Council. And the optimists among us will believe that the Snopeses too will change, and for the better. After all, they will never have the freedom of action the Sartorises had. The great mass of Southerners, white and Negro, may still seem flaccid and inert, willing to leave the shape of the future to those with the loudest voices. But it is a mass finally shaking free of poverty, educating its children, still getting the short end of the nation's bounty but constantly demanding more. It has the power to insist upon better leadership than it has had, in the old days or the new, and in time it will.

CHAPTER 6

OF RED NECKS
AND SILVER TONGUES

THE MOST SPECTACULAR, and perhaps the most significant manifestation of the decline of the Southern aristocratic tradition is to be found in politics. Here, too, the form survived the fact; the manner of the squire still seems to come naturally to the men who occupy the governors' mansions and sit in the Congressional seats, even though many of them owe their success to the calculated exploitation of humble origins.

The great sea change was the direct product of the South's post-Civil War poverty. By the end of the century, growing unrest among the poor whites was translated into resentment against the old Confederates who had been called forth to restore order after the Reconstruction but who seemed incapable of anything more. In the back country there began to be ugly talk that the late unpleasantness had been a rich man's war and a poor man's fight. And there were ambitious and calculating representatives of the new breed at hand to exploit the rising disaffection.

In some of the states the new leaders broke out the banners of Populism and proclaimed a new party. In others they simply took over the existing Democratic machinery, as in South Carolina, where the one-eyed curmudgeon, Ben Tillman, routed the patrician Wade Hampton. It was a political movement which drew its momentum and its color from the mass of poor whites. (Negroes participated only briefly, and significantly in only a few states, before they were summarily disfranchised.) Yet the new crusade was never really out of the control of the rising class of ruling families. The real objects of its wrath were foreign for the most part: the trusts, the Eastern banks, the railroads, all those Yankee moneyed interests which were believed, with cause, to have set their heels upon the neck of the prostrate South. It was a protest movement, with no clear, positive philosophy of its own, held together by a common interest in agriculture that, despite the harsh words, united the largest land-owner and the poorest share-cropper. It produced a few internal reforms, notably the beginning of the present system of public education, and some outstanding public figures—but it also paved the way for the rise of the Southern demagogues.

Still, the outward forms of the old aristocracy survived, even though Southern political institutions began to be shaped by the pressures of direct democracy (Negroes excluded, of course). Ben Tillman might snap his galluses and whittle and spit as he sought votes in the backcountry;

but when he came to town he wore a jim-swinger coat that might have been borrowed from General Hampton, and his manner could only be described as haughty. Indeed, the peak of Tillmanism was marked by a sort of bastardized version of the old *code duello*—the formal notice of intent to kill on sight served by Tillman's office-holding nephew on the editor of the *Columbia State* as a prelude to a fatal shooting.

Thus the many continued to be governed by the few, with the few commonly setting up political dynasties that would survive for many years. The poor whites had a louder voice, and sometimes made it heard in the halls of government; but mainly they relied on the men they sent to Washington or the state capital not only to speak for them, but to tell them what to believe. Their leaders found it wise to maintain the illusion that they were leading a continuing crusade against the old aristocracy—even though as a political force the Virginians were quickly and finally routed. A fair sample of the branchhead oratory of the time is provided by this polemic upon a proposed investigation of one of his antitrust proposals by the redoubtable Governor Jeff Davis of Arkansas:

Whom did they send for, my fellow citizens? Did they send for the laborer; did they send for the manufacturer; did they send for the mechanic; did they send for the merchant; did they send for the class of citizens who bare their breasts and their arms and their backs to the heat and the burdens of the day? No, they sent for the insurance agents from Pine Bluff, from Helena and from Fort Smith. They sent for a high-collared crowd—that crowd that wears collars so high they can't see the sun except over the tops of their collars. They sent for the crowd that, when they shake hands with you, they only give you the tips of two fingers. . . .

This sort of thing outraged and sometimes alarmed those Southerners who professed to gentility, and the demagogues did not go unchallenged. But in order to contest with one of the rural knights, a man had to meet him on his own ground. The voters who gathered on a sultry summer evening for a political meeting demanded red meat and a fair splattering of oratorical blood. They came to hear somebody given hell; the Yankee would do, or Wall Street, or the city folks, and, increasingly in later years, the Negro.

This was perhaps a natural consequence of the lost war and the degeneration of the aristocratic tradition. Even in the days of the Old South's glory, the leadership had enjoined upon its following a defiant and combative stance; since Appomattox the South had had little to be for, and much to be against. Add to this state of mind poverty and widespread ignorance, and a political condition had been created which shaped candidates to its own special requirement.

Some first-class men survived it. They did so by approaching the hustings as a sort of game, and surely many of the voters shared their view. Indeed, in the days when there was nothing to break the monotony of rural life except an occasional visit to the crossroads store and a protracted camp meeting at the churchhouse, political rallies were a prime source of entertainment. They provided a high drama of human conflict, and the principal actors usually played their roles a good deal larger than life. The standard Southern orator may have seemed something of a caricature to more sophisticated audiences, but he was a thespian of no mean attainments.

As a young reporter I had the privilege of watching one of the last of the great stump speakers in action— Cotton Ed Smith of South Carolina. When he finally went to his reward Ed had served 36 continuous years in the United States Senate, standing four-square from first to last upon a three-plank platform: states' rights, tariff for revenue only, and white supremacy. "If it was good enough for John C. Calhoun," he used to say, "it's good enough for me." In 1938 Cotton Ed was at the very top of Franklin D. Roosevelt's ill-starred purge list; the president termed him an obstructionist and formally requested his fellow Democrats not to return him to the Senate. As it turned out this was a break for the senator, who had outraged many South Carolinians by his opposition to the New Deal reforms that had done so much to ease their economic distress. But now he was under fire from a meddling outsider and the role of martyr was one he could play to the hilt.

In those days South Carolina required candidates for state-wide office to appear together in joint debate in each county. Thus the campaign produced a sort of touring stock company, with the principals, their handlers, and the press traveling together through the hot summer months. The production improved as the run continued. From the beginning Ed referred to his leading opponent, former Governor Olin Johnston, as "Brother Oleander" and to the secondary contender, State Senator Edgar Brown, as "Satchel Edgar." One inspired evening he arose after Brown, who had promised more and bigger WPA projects, to toss off of his capacious cuff this devastating line: "Satchel Edgar says if you send him to Washington he will bring home the bacon. I have only one question: To whose home?"

But Ed's masterpiece was The Philadelphia Story. So far as I know this was never set down verbatim at the time and the following rendition is based on my memory, and that of Turner Catledge, the managing editor of *The New York Times*, who heard it as a reporter and has always regarded it as a gem never surpassed even in his native Mississippi. The Story was Ed's version of his famous bolt from the Democratic National Convention two years before when a Negro minister had appeared on the platform to pray.

"I have been trying to keep this campaign on a high plane," Ed would proclaim as he paced the flat bed of a cotton truck. "It has been my custom to start out with the Magna Charta and trace the long history of the struggle for human rights. But the other night, up yonder in Pickens County, I had started out with the fields of Runnymede and proceeded to the point where I had the boys in gray halfway up the hill at Gettysburg, when an old man in the front row spit out his tobacco cud and said, 'Hell, Ed, tell us about Phillydelphy.'

"So I told them. I told them about walking up to that great convention hall, and being stopped there at the outer door—the outer door, mind you—by a stranger who demanded to see my credentials. 'Young man,' I said, 'if we have reached a time when the senior senator from South Carolina has to have credentials to get into a Democratic convention, I don't want in.' And he stepped aside.

"But when I came out on the floor of that great hall, bless God, it looked like a checkerboard—a spot of white here, and a spot of black there. But I kept going, down that long aisle, and finally I found the great standard of South Carolina—and, praise God, it was in a spot of white!

"I had no sooner than taken my seat when a newspaperman came down the aisle and squatted down by me and said, 'Senator, did you know a nigger is going to come out up yonder in a minute and offer the invocation?' I told him, I said, 'Now don't be joking me, I'm upset enough the way it is.' But then, bless God, out on that platform walked a slew-footed, blue-gummed, kinky-headed Senegambian!

"And he started praying and I started walking. And as I pushed through those great doors, and walked across that vast rotunda, it seemed to me that old John Calhoun leaned down from his mansion in the sky and whispered in my ear, 'You did right, Ed. . . .'"

The Philadelphia Story had all the basic ingredients, and it carried the senator along to a victory climaxed by a stirring scene on election night when, with honest tears coursing into his grizzled moustache, he posed for photographers on the statehouse grounds wearing the red shirt of Reconstruction and clutching the rear leg of Wade Hampton's bronze charger. I suppose the Story shocked many of the outlanders who heard it, or read about it; and certainly the success of the run was a grievous disappointment to Franklin Roosevelt. Yet to the initiated, to the orators and to the audience, there was a sort of innocence about it. The white men who gathered under the chinaberry trees to whoop and holler as Ed built his climaxes didn't really object to being prayed over by a Senegambian, and didn't believe Ed did either. And, most remarkable of all, nobody enjoyed the performance more than the Negroes who stood, white teeth gleaming in the dark, at the rear of the crowd. "Hot damn," they would chortle, "Old Ed's pourin' it on tonight. . . ."

The real significance of the Philadelphia Story, I think, was its magnificent irrelevance. South Carolina was perhaps as hard hit by the depression as any state in the union; recovery was painfully slow from the collapse of prices and credit. Even in 1938 baled cotton still stood under the trees along the back roads waiting for a market, short shifts in the cotton mills drained the economy of the Piedmont factory towns, and in the cities long lines of whites and blacks queued at the relief stations for oranges and bacon. South Carolina's real problems lay in the red soil that washed down to rivers that had never been harnessed—in the depletion and neglect of its natural resources, and the corresponding erosion of its human resources. Yet on those hot nights under the flickering lights, these matters were not meaningfully discussed; and in fairness it should be noted that the audience probably would have been offended had an orator, instead of spinning dreams of past glory to assuage its misery, sug-

gested that perhaps something was fundamentally wrong
with the Southern Way of Life.

I suppose Cotton Ed would have to be classified as a
demagogue by any standard definition. Yet his sins were
of omission, not of commission. I don't think he intended
to inflame his followers, or launch them on any course of
action beyond that necessary to return him to office. I
doubt that he ever sought deliberately to mislead them.
It was my feeling that he came to enjoy his performance
as much as his audience, as any good actor does, and
perhaps even to believe in the role he played; the oratory,
with its ghostly hoofbeats of Confederate cavalry, was an
end in itself without any direct relationship to what he
would do once he was safely returned to Washington—
which would be nothing much.

This, of course, was not true of all of those who learned
to successfully ring changes on the time-tested theme.
There were thin-lipped, hating men among them; the
elder Talmadge of Georgia and Bilbo of Mississippi were
conspicuous examples, and the contemporary Eastland fits
the pattern. It is, for example, a long distance in spirit if
not in text from Cotton Ed's charge up the hill at Gettysburg to Jim Eastland's solemn call to the Mississippi
Association of Citizens Councils to subvert the government of the United States:

The anti-segregation decisions are dishonest decisions. Although rendered by judges whose sworn duty it was to up-
hold the law and to protect and preserve the constitution of
the United States, these decisions were dictated by political

pressure groups bent upon the destruction of the American system of government, and the mongrelization of the white race. The judges who rendered them violated their oaths of office. They have disgraced the high office they hold. The court has responded to a radical pro-Communist political movement in this country. . . . We in the South cannot stay longer on the defensive. This is the road to destruction and death. We must take the offense. . . .

Even if one concedes Eastland's sincerity, in the context of this troubled time he stands indicted of gross irresponsibility. There is no echo of Confederate bugles here; the ghost evoked by these reckless words is that of the latter-day Ku Klux Klansman, armed with rope and faggot, stalking his prey outside the law.

Still, as I have suggested, this florid framework of one-party Southern campaigning has not finally established its own Gresham's law in which the bad candidate inevitably drives out the good. For one thing, it has been, until very recent years, a highly individual business. There were rural courthouse rings, and some of the cities—most notably Memphis—provided local political machines of the standard American type. But most of the titans built their careers on an intensely personal following. An old hand in North Carolina once gave me an estimate I believe applied in most of the states: roughly one-quarter of the votes, he figured, could be bought, and another quarter could be delivered by negotiation with local leaders; but at least half had to be persuaded. The persuading, of course, had to be done in person, from the stump.

Within the limits of the thespian tradition, a man had a fair amount of leeway. Many of the best practitioners avoided the race issue entirely, or soft-pedaled it when their opponents tossed it on the fire. When it came time for hell-giving they could always use the Republican Party and Herbert Hoover without any undue strain on their Democratic consciences. And, once past the first test of a fire-breathing campaign, a canny man, making skillful use of his patronage and franking privilege, could stay in office a long time. I recall a note of envy in the comment of Senator Paul Douglas of Illinois upon receipt of the intelligence that the Democratic ticket had closed in Arkansas, for the second senatorial election in a row, with no name on it except that of J. William Fulbright. "Tell him," Douglas sighed, "that he is not only a scholar and a gentleman, but he is the first politician in the land."

The political longevity of Southern members of Congress, indeed, has been a source of concern to their colleagues from other sections of the country. It enables them to sharpen their parliamentary skills, and under the seniority system it moves them steadily up the ladder to control of the vital House and Senate committees in the seasons of Democratic majority. When the Southerners join in a solid front, which they do upon any issue touching upon race, they can usually bottle up any bill, or worry it to death with a filibuster. Their annual success in the case of civil rights legislation has created a false image of the Southern bloc, which is loosely identified as Dixiecrat and regarded as uniformly conservative.

Yet when one sets the race issue aside and examines the voting records of the Southern congressmen, a considerable variety emerges. Like most of their colleagues their

votes are colored by the interests of their constituents;
but as it happens, in several important areas this has
tended to line them up on the liberal side of the aisle. In
matters of resource conservation, and most notably public
power, they have been generally aligned with the re-
formers of the West. Southerners took the lead in the
original rural electric cooperative movement, and the
"creeping socialism" of TVA has drawn its support not
only from such professed Southern liberals as Estes Kefauver, but from mavericks like Theodore Bilbo. Cotton
Ed Smith fathered the original farm price support legislation, which, whatever else it may be, is a far cry from
Adam Smith; John Sparkman of Alabama is a leading
advocate of public housing; Wright Patman of Texas is
perhaps the House's most constant critic of the banking
interests; Richard Russell of Georgia considers the free
school lunch program one of his major monuments; Lister
Hill of Alabama has led the battle for federal aid to education. And while it is true that a majority of the Southerners are less prone to go along with pro-labor legislation
than their colleagues from states where the unions have
greater political influence, there are those among them,
like Olin Johnston of South Carolina, who make a profes-
sion of being a friend of the workingman.

But it is in another essential test of the contemporary
liberal faith that the Southern delegations, until very recent years, have measured up far more consistently than
the representatives of other sections of the country. Indeed, from the days of Grover Cleveland forward, it has
been the solid Southern vote that in every critical test has

kept the nation from succumbing to the virus of isolation-ism. Without the Southerners, Woodrow Wilson could not have led the country into World War I, nor could Franklin Roosevelt have made the necessary commitments that kept Great Britain a bastion against Nazi Germany and finally put the United States in the field. Between the wars the Southerners stood with Wilson on the League of Nations issue almost to a man; and they were counted among the moving spirits that founded the United Nations and went on to fight for the Truman program of Communist containment. And in a logical extension of Calhoun's old demand for tariff for revenue only, they have been the nation's most consistent advocates of free trade; it is no accident that the reciprocal trade program stands as a monument to a Tennessean, Cordell Hull. It was the disproportionate strength of Southern influence that kept the Democratic Party internationalist throughout its history, and thereby drew the most consistent and perhaps the most significant dividing line between the two major parties.

It can be argued with justice that this was a reflection of the region's self-interest; the South's two great crops, cotton and tobacco, have depended upon export markets and have been in trouble since foreign trade began to wither in the Thirties. Yet, whatever the motive, I believe that history has demonstrated that in this vital area the South has been a benign influence on the Republic. And if I am correct in this view, one of the most alarming trends of the day is the visible shifting of the Southern political position on foreign policy.

This is, of course, related to the shift in Southern economic interest. The old devotion to free trade was the product of an agrarian society, although it was undoubtedly colored by a sentimental sense of identification with the British cousins overseas. But comparable ties of blood and sentiment did not blind the old New England manufacturers to the need for protective tariffs to build a wall between American markets and the cotton mills of Manchester. Today the greatest concentration of cotton textile production in the nation is in the Piedmont South—and my Cousin Robert, perhaps to the discomfort of the ghost of an earlier Ashmore who held the same congressional seat in South Carolina's secession delegation, casts his vote on tariff matters with the assorted Republicans and Democrats from Massachusetts.

Tradition, and for many, a natural inclination, still holds a majority of the Southerners to the international line on foreign policy. Yet the conservatives whose instinct urges them away from large financial commitments for foreign aid now encounter little public opposition in the South if they care to reverse their field. In the post-World War II years, Walter George of Georgia was the senior apostle of internationalism in the Senate. But when he bowed to the inevitable and decided not to stand for re-election, he was replaced by Herman Talmadge, who has carried his race-inspired preoccupation with states' rights over to support of the isolationist Bricker Amendment; surely one of the most remarkable sounds of our time is the soft Talmadge drawl alternating with the Midwest twang of Clarence

Manion in an approving radio discussion of what amounts to the old America First program.

Increasingly nowadays Southern congressmen in their dissertations before the home folks are applying a new equation to foreign aid. They wonder out loud if we should be pouring tax money into a high dam in Pakistan when we haven't yet developed the Arkansas, the Ouachita, and the Red; if we should be spending American cash to clean up the British and French mess in the Suez Canal when the harbor at Mobile needs attention. No one is yet advocating Fortress America; but a substantial number are launched on a course of logic that seems to lead to it.

Public opinion in the South is not pushing the leadership to this position, but, as I have suggested, it is no longer holding the leadership back. The mass of Southerners for the first time are making enough money to be troubled by taxes, and they share the growing national obsession with a reduction in the federal budget. And the old counterbalance of agrarian economic interest is constantly losing weight; the cotton farmers, in truth, no longer have much hope of again placing their surplus crops in foreign markets instead of government warehouses. At this point in the transition, the leadership could, I believe, take the constituency either way on foreign policy. But the fact seems to be that the Southern leaders—some in disgusted reaction to the vacillations of the Eisenhower administration, others in a natural reversion to their basic parochialism—are rapidly losing the keen edge of their old internationalist fervor.

I have dealt here primarily with the national figures, the Southerners who go forth to do battle in the great arena at Washington. They are, I think, the best of the local political breed, and I suggest that in any dispassionate measurement of their collective capacity (this presupposes setting the race issue aside) they would rate well above the average in either house of Congress. V. O. Key, Jr., author of the definitive *Southern Politics*, has taken note of how well and responsibly the bulk of the Southerners behaved in that time when the fever of McCarthyism racked the nation. It is true, as some cynics have suggested, that they were uniquely fitted by personal experience to recognize a demagogue when they saw one; but Key thought he also saw surviving signs of the old aristocratic

tendency to regard the responsibilities of governance more as the guardianship of a patrimony than as the duty of a corporation lawyer—or a walking delegate—to use the means at hand, whether fair or foul, to advance the momentary interests of his client. . . .

In any case the Jeffersonian strain of political doctrine runs more strongly in Mississippi than in, let us say, Ohio. After all, Mr. Jefferson served his apprenticeship in what would today be called a Southern county courthouse gang.

Further down the scale, however, I am afraid Key's verdict does not stand up. The South has had, and has, some first-rate governors—men of vision who understand the nature of the challenge posed by the great changes rushing upon their states. Yet they are, without any significant exception I can think of, constantly handicapped and harassed by their legislatures. Indeed, the running conflict between those who are elected statewide and those who represent local interests has become another symbol of the transition from the Old South to the New.

State government everywhere in the nation is usually the weakest link in the chain from local community to federal capital. But in the South it bears the special handicap of disproportionate representation between rural areas, which everywhere are rapidly losing population, and urban areas, which everywhere are gaining. The South's future, its problems, and its most pressing needs lie in the cities now—yet, as in the classic case of Georgia, where the county unit system gives Atlanta virtually no voice in the legislature, the cities are the orphans of the state government.

The legislatures have become the happy hunting grounds of the interests. The typical member is a small town lawyer who makes no secret of the fact that he has accepted a part-time job that pays little in salary or prestige in order to run errands for his clients. There are usually well-defined and openly recognized blocs ready to do the bidding of utilities, liquor dealers, insurance companies, banks, labor unions, or any other enterprise which wants something from the state, or wants the state to let it alone. When a governor wants to put through a state tax program for improved services he knows exactly where he has to start trading, with whom, and for what.

In these legislative bear pits the Southern political system has reached its lowest ebb. Here even the outward forms of decorum are more often ignored than observed;

as the saying goes, you can't tell a member from a lobbyist without a score card. It is not so much outright corruption —although there is enough of that—as it is a sort of unholy meshing of public and private interests without any effective restraint from an electorate bemused by other, perhaps in fact more important, matters. About the best any governor can hope to do is keep the interests in fair balance.

In my more optimistic moments I have the feeling that this too is bound to change with the rest. But in the long hours I have spent watching the manifestations of grass-roots government in the legislative halls, it has seemed to me a marvelous thing that states' rights have survived as long and as well as they have. And I have wondered, too, if those who advocate the Bricker Amendment and its companion pieces have ever paused to consider what would really happen if, in this nervous age of the split atom, we gave full voice in the conduct of the nation's foreign affairs to Representative Snopes of Yoknapatawpha County.

CHAPTER 7

COMPUTATIONS ON
A BALANCE SHEET

IT IS A singular fact that the Old South, with its aristocratic pretensions to learning and culture, produced
no men of letters above the rank of the minor poet,
Sidney Lanier, and the novelist, William Gilmore Sims.
It is even more noteworthy that the New South has seen
a literary boom that matches and may even surpass its
economic renascence.

I do not intend to join here with the critics who are
bemused by the fact that the most illiterate state in the
union has turned out an astounding collection of resident
and expatriate poets, playwrights, and novelists. There
may be some occult significance in the fact that the
literature of New England flowered early and then went
to seed despite the continued development of that region's
ivied seats of learning. And it could be argued, I suppose,
that what has happened in Mississippi has been more in

the nature of a deflowering—that the artists who poke among the ruins of the old feudal society are inspired by the special aura of decadence rather than a formal pursuit of the masters.

Whatever the cause, there can be no doubt that Mississippi has an unusually high per capita incidence of writers who manage to make a living at their trade. There is, first of all (and perhaps for posterity first and last), William Faulkner. The Oxford recluse is so accomplished a craftsman that the critics, despite an assiduous effort back in the Thirties, have found that they simply cannot ignore him, and now he has received the international accolade of a Nobel Prize. Spun off, in a sense, by Faulkner's enormous talent (not consciously, certainly, for if there is a Faulkner school the master does not attend it), there are such odd and special practitioners as Tennessee Williams and Truman Capote. In a remote sphere of her own there is the talented lady, Eudora Welty. And this roll call could be continued to include another dozen or so whose works would have to be included in any sampling of serious American literature.

As I have suggested elsewhere, it seems to me that Faulkner has spoken important truths about the nature of Southern society. Yet, so far, his has generally been a backward view; he has been primarily concerned with how Yoknapatawpha got the way it is. And since he has chosen to frame a universal human tragedy within a social microcosm, those who attempt to interpret the broader Southern scene in Faulkner's dimensions are subject to an inevitable distortion. Indeed, when Faulkner himself departs from his concern with the central conflict between good and evil and deals with transient matters, he displays a sort of tortured naïvete. In his occasional letters to the editor of the Memphis *Commercial Appeal*, and in a fragmented article in *Harper's*, he seems to argue that the South's concern over desegregation is largely economic— the possible loss of a pool of exploitable labor and with it the rise of new competition for the dollars now flowing freely in the region. He writes of ". . . the tawdry quality of the fear—fear not of the Negro as an individual Negro nor even as a race, but as an economic class or stratum or factor, since what the Negro threatens is not the white man's social system but the southern white man's economic system. . . ."

This would seem to align Faulkner with the economic determinists, which is strange company indeed for a man who in his fiction treats so profoundly with the complexities of the Southern mind. I suppose there are in Mississippi and elsewhere in the South still a good many planters who are interested in keeping the Negro in his place primarily as a guarantee of an adequate supply of cheap field labor. But I must say it has been a long time since I have met one who even discussed the race problem in these terms. Indeed, down in the Delta country where the tractors and the giant, spiderlike cotton pickers snort across the black land, there is more likely to be talk of the problem of keeping the hands busy. And now along the highways of the Mississippi Valley there moves a remarkable parade of battered trucks filled with dry-backs —Mexican migratory workers brought across the border on legal contract to work their way north through the planting season and back south again with the cotton harvest. A friend of mine, who as late as ten years ago kept sixty families on his two thousand acres to get his cotton crop down and bring it in, now has only three. He has transferred some of his acreage to beef cattle pasturage, and he handles the rest with machinery, chemicals, and day labor.

It seems to me, then, that the Mississippi literary view is not only special, but somewhat out of date. I am not suggesting that the ruined plantation house Tennessee Williams employed as a stage set in the celebrated movie *Baby Doll* doesn't exist; but I am suggesting that the problem of arson among the cotton gins is not one that personally concerns many Southerners these days. While *Baby Doll* may have been accepted as a slice of life outside the region, it was generally viewed in the South as comedy; twenty years ago *Tobacco Road* evoked cries that Erskine Caldwell was fouling his nest, but Williams' saga of an infantile blonde and her frustrated husband drew belly laughs. Even the Southern censors didn't bother it much, although this may have been accounted for by automatic Protestant approval in the wake of Cardinal Spellman's censure.

Considering *Baby Doll* and its relationship to contemporary life under the magnolias, Harry Golden in his *Carolina Israelite* has offered this substitute scenario outline as being closer to the mark:

I would have Eli Wallach play the role of a manufacturer of ladies' foundation garments; slips and brassieres, with a factory on West 36th Street and Seventh Avenue. The International Ladies Garment Workers Union is after him to sign a new contract and Eli (like so many hundreds of others) decides to clear out of New York. He makes arrangements for a new factory in the magnolia-scented town of Kenilworth, South Carolina, where the folks are raising a half-million dollars to provide Eli with the new factory building.

To throw the union off the track, Eli calls his new brassiere factory "Balance Agriculture with Industry, Incorporated," but he has made one big mistake. He has recently promoted Baby Doll, his former model, to a fifty per cent partnership in his business and she is now following him down to Kenilworth in her new Jaguar. And this is where old Karl Malden comes in. Karl plays David Dubinsky, who has been keeping an eye on Baby Doll all this time, and he catches up with her in Charlotte, North Carolina. They play hide and seek in an old plantation house which now houses *The Carolina Israelite,* and in the scuffle Dubinsky succeeds in getting Baby Doll to sign the new contract on behalf of "Balance Agriculture with Industry, Incorporated."

The big scene, however, is where the Mayor of Kenilworth is dedicating the new factory:

"We are mighty proud of the new factory, Mr. Eli, and on behalf of all your good neighbors of Kenilworth I hereby hand you this certificate which makes your company rent-free, water-free, power-free and tax-free for the first five years of your operations; and one thing more, Mr. Eli, and I'm certainly mighty proud to be able to say this to you-all—we are a very peaceful little town here with no trouble and you can be sure of one thing—you'll never be bothered by them union fellows down here. . . ."

Just then Baby Doll rushes onto the grandstand, followed by David Dubinsky, who waves the newly-signed union contract and shouts into the loud-speaker: *"We start picketing tomorrow!"*

The fact is that the dominant economic interests in the New South—granting a few local exceptions—not only are not engaged in any calculated effort to keep the Negro in his place, but are providing a significant counterbalance for the incendiary activities of the Citizens Councils and the reborn Klans. It is not that the bustling gentlemen at the local Chambers of Commerce or the state Industrial Development Commissions are particularly concerned with race as a moral problem; on the contrary, they, like most of their fellow Southerners, wish the matter of integration would quietly go away, and many of them privately share the views of the Councilmen and the Klux. But they also recognize that sustained racial disorder would be fatal to their effort to lure new industries and new capital from the non-South, and that the existing level of tension isn't doing their handsomely mounted promotional campaigns any good.

A few weeks before the 1954 Supreme Court ruling in the school cases I paid a call on a Southern business executive who likes to be described as the sparkplug of his state's increasingly successful drive to balance agriculture with industry. He had expended much money and energy in the cause and had expounded the gospel across the melted ice cream of a thousand luncheon club tables, at home and in the money markets of the East—the story of vast natural resources and a docile, hard-working labor supply waiting only for the touch of Yankee investment capital to send milk and honey flowing through the land.

I asked him if he had given any thought to the possible effect of the pending Supreme Court ruling on his industrial development program. He said he hadn't, much. Suppose, I said, the Court rules out segregation in the schools?

"Good God," he said. "You mean they might?"

I told him I thought the odds were that they would, and that this, of course, raised the possibility of racial violence in the South. He sprang from his chair and began pacing.

"We can't have it," he said, his voice rising. "My God, if the Klan starts riding again and kicking nigras around my company couldn't borrow fifty cents in Wall Street. And nobody in his right mind would build a plant in a town where people are throwing dynamite at each other.

"One lynching," he continued, still pacing, "and we've wasted two hundred thousand dollars in magazine advertising. The Northern press will be running stories that make it sound like the Civil War has started all over again. Hell, what we've been selling is peace and order—telling 'em that what we've got down here is stability—friendly politicians who are not going to gut a business with taxes, and workers who are grateful for a job and are not going to be stirring up trouble."

What, then, did he propose to do about it? Would he and his fellow industrialists in the region consider joining in a public statement urging orderly compliance with the Court's decision? He sat down and thought a moment.

"We're not going to want to get mixed up in this school thing if we can help it," he said. "But I can tell you this —there're not going to be any race riots."

And there haven't been. Mean talk, yes. Isolated acts of

individual violence, as in the Till case; an occasional mob such as the one that formed to bar Autherine Lucy from the University of Alabama, or the one at Little Rock which, after three weeks of solicitation by Governor Faubus, overwhelmed the local police at Central High School; a stick of dynamite tossed on a Negro leader's porch. Deplorable as this may be, it falls far short of organized forays into Negro neighborhoods to burn, pillage, and murder on a wholesale scale. With far more real provocation than existed a generation ago when such affairs were commonplace, there has not been a single lynching in the grand manner—the sort of fiesta where an entire community gathers, children and all, to watch the crosses burn and the limp body sway at the end of the rope.

It might be contended that this is negative, that the difference is only one of degree and that the distinction is between physical and spiritual torture. Yet it is a matter, I think, of considerable significance. For what it means is that the power structure of the South has declared outright violence and sustained disorder intolerable and will use its great weight to prevent it if it can, and to curb it if it can't. Where prominent citizens participate openly in the activities of the Citizens Councils, as in Mississippi and some parts of Alabama, they have made this a condition of membership and have given it more than lip service. Elsewhere in the South the established leaders have generally stayed clear of the extremist groups— making no overt move to curb the rabble rousers, but letting it be known that they will be tolerated only so long as they stay within somewhat elastic bounds that stop short of anything the meddling, outside newspapers could call an incident. Thus Governor Frank Clement had virtually universal support when he sent the Tennessee National Guard to halt the rioting incited by itinerant racists in the wake of integration of the Clinton public schools. Tennesseans who felt strongly that the schools shouldn't admit Negroes now, or ever, agreed that there had to be order; they might defend an economic boycott on moral grounds, but they couldn't put up with brawling in the streets. So it was at Nashville. The leaders of the business community displayed no particular alarm when John Kasper roamed the streets preaching sedition and a few Negro children were pushed around on the opening day of school; but when a half million dollars worth of public property disappeared in the dynamiting of the Hattie Cotton School the word went out that this sort of thing had to stop, and the local police stopped it. At Little Rock the first break in the silence that fell over the business community when Governor Faubus pitted the National Guard against the Federal Court came after the financial gentry had actually gazed upon the face of a mob; twenty-six community leaders, whose ratings would place them in the upper reaches of Dun & Bradstreet's compilation of the American peerage, thereupon issued a public statement demanding the restoration of law and order.

If economic determinism were the sole factor, which of course it isn't, the rigid patterns of segregation would have been shattered long ago. Just as the mass of white Southerners had no financial stake in the slave system, so the great majority today draws no benefit from the exist-

ence of a mass of workers forced by necessity to hire out
for substandard wages. The South's traditional poverty has
been rooted in the fact that the colored third of the
region's population, and a substantial portion of those of
lighter hue, have been counted among the lowest income
group in the nation. This pool of cheap labor has turned a
real profit only for those engaged in large-scale farming
or the manufacture of products for sale outside the South;
for the rest it has been a major economic handicap. To
wholesalers and retailers of consumer goods, to those who
operate the service trades, to professional men and women,
it has meant a local market far below the potential indicated when national income averages are measured
against Southern census figures. And it has added to the
general burden, since those with marginal incomes contribute little in the way of tax support for public services,
yet draw heavily upon them. It was economics, not mo-
rality, Booker T. Washington had in mind when he warned
that the white man could throw the Negro in the ditch,
but couldn't keep him there without getting in with him.

These truths have long been recognized, but rarely
acted upon. The change, when it began in the post-de-
pression days, came not a result of the concerted efforts
of the Southern leadership, but from the external actions
of the central government. The federal wage and hour
law produced profound results in the region. So, to a
lesser degree, did the social security and unemployment
insurance programs. Together they have served to raise
the accepted standards of subsistence, and to push a mass
of new consumers up above the fatback-and-hominy level.

The flood of defense spending when the army camps burgeoned in the South during World War II, and the new surge of industrial expansion have kept the spiral turning; the national journals that deal in merchandising data are filled with reports of the astronomical growth of Southern retail markets. I can recall as a young reporter riding through the back country of South Carolina with a public health team administering the new miracle drug, nicotinic acid, as a treatment for the common scourge, pellagra—that scaling disease which results from sustained dietary deficiencies. The only case of pellagra I have heard of in recent years afflicted an alcoholic of my acquaintance who had largely given up food, not because he couldn't afford it, but because he could afford to stay drunk. Negroes as well as whites are not only eating higher on the hog than ever before, but they have money left over for television sets, automobiles, fur coats, deep freezes, and all the other luxuries Americans regard as necessities.

The average Negro income is still well below that of the whites, but it is high enough to make an increasing number of colored people good customers of almost any establishment along Main Street. In some cases the Negro has even achieved a special priority; because the patterns of residential segregation normally restrict him to second-class housing regardless of income, the outward symbol of his affluence is likely to be a long, chromium-studded, new automobile rather than a pretentious home. Indeed, proprietors of shops which once barred Negroes or asked them to ease in through the alley door, are likely these days to be out hustling colored customers in off the sidewalk; I know one clothing merchant who considers his membership in the Urban League a better investment than his Chamber of Commerce dues. The ebony radio stations which have sprung up in the Southern cities to beam programs especially to Negro audiences peddle most of their commercial time to leading white stores. And some department store owners, taking due note of the complexion of the crowds moving through their aisles, have quietly taken down the White and Colored signs that adorned their drinking fountains—although in almost every instance the toilets still remain strongholds of white supremacy.

This has been a quiet and undramatic process, more the natural product of a competitive economy than the result of organized effort on the part of Negroes; they have found doors opening to them simply because they arrive these days with money in hand. However, in the case of public transportation economic weight has been used as a direct weapon against segregation. The bus boycott in Montgomery succeeded despite the fulminations of white politicians and the odd legalisms of the local courts because the bus company had to carry Negro passengers or go out of business. In every Southern city the proportion of colored bus riders far exceeds the general proportion of Negro to white population, commonly running up as high as 80 per cent. Under the circumstances it does not take a full-scale boycott to remind the proprietors where their profit lies; even a moderate decline in colored passengers would be enough to force most of the hard-pressed transit companies to the wall. This is the primary consideration that has moved some twenty-one Southern bus operators to quietly take down the Jim Crow signs without court order.

The Negro's new economic leverage has not yet become anything like a determinant in the area of social attitudes; but by indirection it has, I believe, provided an effective brake on the extremist groups. For the first time he is a positive rather than a negative factor in the Southern economy, and the urban business community is becoming aware that when a colored man becomes a customer it is a practical necessity to take some account of his personal feelings. And here again this is a beginning process that will not be turned back. Winthrop Rockefeller, who has established a branch of his well-endowed clan atop an Arkansas mountain and assumed the chairmanship of the state Industrial Development Commission, has set as a goal the raising of Arkansas's 47th ranking per capita income to the national average. The Negro inevitably must be included in this calculation. He may be the last to find a job at the machines of the new factories, but clearly his income has got to rise with the others' if the goal is to be attained—and if the Arkansas businessmen who support the promotional effort are to get a fair return on their investment through expanded local markets.

It should be noted, too, that this new economic crusade differs in important respects from that of Henry Grady's day. These are not innocents from the pulpit and the plantation who are now out stalking new factories, nor are they passing the tambourine for small local donations. In most cases the promotional effort is financed in large part by a substantial state budget, and allied with the professional greeters are platoons of economists and engineers from the state universities. They are happy to see local ownership of industry and they will be as helpful to the homefolks as they can; but their main effort is directed at the East and Mid-West. They recognize that the South is still painfully short of risk capital, and that its economic development depends primarily upon the great national corporations and the expanding smaller companies seeking plant sites outside the older industrial concentrations. So they go forth not to plead for help, but to make the hard sell, and they arm themselves with resource surveys, labor availability data, market analyses, and the like. At home they bend their efforts to creating what they fondly describe as a favorable climate for industry. This may mean, at its extreme, tax exemptions, publicly-financed factory buildings, and right-to-work laws aimed at curbing the unions. On both ends, then, this is not a moral crusade but Operation Self-Interest—which, I suspect, largely accounts for its remarkable success.

I would not describe as cold-blooded the gentlemen with the slide rules who are plotting the shape of the South's future, but I would call them realistic. Thus they count racial tension as a debit, and general improvement of the condition of the South's Negroes as an asset. They are not disposed to mount any stumps and meet the Citizens Councilmen in debate on the great moral issue, but they do keep a close eye on the profit and loss sheet. In Birmingham the former chairman of the Chamber of Commerce's Committee of 100 commented tersely on the

Citizens Council-inspired violence on local buses: "The hoodlumism here has hit headlines throughout the nation. As a result, we have lost one major plant in Birmingham and several smaller installations." He was echoed by the Alabama Power Company vice-president in charge of industrial development. And the *Birmingham Post-Herald* said: "This points up the necessity for our public officials to apprehend and bring to trial those persons who have been guilty of this violence." The power structure had been alerted—as it was in Arkansas when Orval Faubus suddenly gave signs of bedding down with the Citizens Councilmen he had previously resisted. Two days before the governor launched his military maneuver at Central High School, Winthrop Rockefeller got wind of what was afoot and descended from his mountain to plead with Faubus not to do it. After it was done, Rockefeller read into the record of a national television broadcast his own appraisal (which it is reasonable to assume is also that of the Rockefeller Brothers and the Chase Manhattan Bank) that great damage had been done to Arkansas's industrial development program.

The promoters keep an eye on the future, too. Right now the South's greatest single asset in its competition for new industry probably is its possession of the nation's only supply of surplus labor—a sizable pool not of unemployed, but underemployed workers in transition from farm to city. In any community in the South a new factory can start from scratch and fill a thousand jobs the day its doors open. Those who turn up to man the machines are not skilled workers, but they can be quickly trained; and the efficiency ratings of companies that have already gone through the process are impressive. However, the supply is not inexhaustible. The time will come, sooner or later, when the factories will have skimmed the whites off the labor pool and only the blacks will be left—and, assuming the demand continues, there is little doubt that this will be the beginning of the end of rigid segregation patterns in employment. This consideration opens up an area of concern for those who look as far ahead as day after tomorrow. When former Governor Sam Jones of Louisiana propounds his thesis of a forced redistribution of Negroes over the whole of the United States as a cure for the race problem, he may draw a few emotional huzzahs, but he is likely to alarm the slide rule gentry. They see in the present out-migration of Negroes the dissipation of a work force that may soon be a magnet for the factories they seek, and of a potential market for Southern manufactured goods. And the more thoughtful among them are also aware that the qualitative loss may be far greater than the cold census figures indicate; it is usually the ablest and most ambitious Negroes who put their foot in the big road to seek greater opportunity or to escape oppression, thus running up the proportion, among those who stay behind, of those who can best be described by that explicit Southern word, shiftless.

Although the industrial promoters and the labor unions are often at cross purposes, they have a common stake in preserving order and reducing racial tension. Organizing in the South has always been tough, and the percentage of workers covered by union contract is the lowest in the nation. The first of the New Southern industries, the cotton mills of the Piedmont, were antilabor bastions from the outset. They were usually located in unincorporated towns, where the proprietors literally owned the streets that led to them and paid the policemen who patrolled them. And when a concerted effort was made by the organizers to break through the cordon—as in the days of the old Textile Workers Organizing Committee's flying squadrons of the Thirties—the mill owners could rely on their friends in the statehouses for help. I was around the villages myself then as a reporter in the hectic days when Mother Bloor was likely to turn up on the picket line and Norman Thomas would appear to preach the funeral oration for pickets shot down in the line of duty. I have a sharp memory of the long cyclone fences and the sandbags neatly stacked at the gates with the blunt snouts of National Guard machine-guns poking through.

That sort of copper-plated resistance has diminished sharply with the national shifting of political balance in the unions' favor; but the organizers still have their troubles. Operation Dixie, the CIO's all-out Southern drive in the post-war years, fell flat on its face, and the rate of increase in membership since has by no means kept pace with the growth of industry. The new Southern factory workers, lately come in from the country, have a deep-seated suspicion of the persuasive strangers who ask them to sign up for the union. And it is a suspicion usually encouraged by their employers, many of whom come South, if not in the hope of permanently escaping organization, at least with the hope that they can hold it off for a few years and negotiate a far more favorable contract than the one they left behind.

In the last few years racial tensions have had an increasingly adverse effect upon organizing campaigns. The union internationals, without significant exception, formally oppose segregation, and their charters declare their membership open without regard to race. The Southern locals, however, have been reluctant to follow suit; there is nothing in the act of signing a union card to cause a man to abandon the prejudices he has lived with all his life, and the unions recruit their members mostly from the ranks of the red-necks who nurse a special bitterness. It was no surprise that the mob that chased Autherine Lucy off the University of Alabama campus included a heavy percentage of dues-paying rubber workers, or that there were Teamsters and railway workers among those present in Little Rock. And it must be a source of continuing embarrassment to Walter Reuther that Eldon Lee Edwards, the imperial wizard of the Knights of the Ku Klux Klan, carries a card in the Atlanta local of the United Auto Workers.

It is not likely, however, that the unions will abandon or significantly temper their aggressive campaign to educate their Southern members not only to accept integration in the factories, but to play a positive role in breaking down the general barriers of race. Primarily this undertaking has been within the province of the Political Action Committee, which has sought to increase labor's local political strength by coupling it with the Negro vote. The PAC's outriders point out, with justice, that allied with the Citizens Councils and the Klux are reactionary employer groups perhaps more interested in undermining the unions than in keeping the Negro in his place. This, too, is basically an appeal to self-interest, and the internationals have no choice but to stay with it even though some of the locals have grown restive over the race issue and a few have threatened to turn in their charters.

It seems to me, then, that wherever money makes the mare go the odds are with the Negro—and a mare is a considerably more dependable animal than a mule given to running into stone walls either because he is blind or doesn't give a damn. It is commonly said that some of the best minds in the South have rallied to the effort to fend off the effects of the Supreme Court integration decisions —and this is true to the extent that some able advocates have helped the politicians work out the legal maze of interposition. But there are able minds poring over the balance sheet, too, and while they are willing to put up with a good deal of nonsense, they aren't willing to pay cash for it.

Thus the Mississippi Sovereignty Commission, brought into being by the 1956 legislature to keep the Magnolia State free of any taint of integration, and supplied with $250,000 of public money for the purpose, collapsed in its first direct test against the outside dollar. The issue was the proposed erection of an $11,000,000 Veterans Administration Hospital at Jackson, a facility that would accept white and Negro patients alike and house them together without distinction. "Well, we've got the tiger by the tail," Governor Coleman said. "We either accept an integrated facility, or we deny our Mississippi white veterans medical services they need." With only one dissenting voice the Commission voted to donate state land for the hospital.

One does not have to be an economic determinist to find merit in the thesis advanced by a somewhat cynical old planter I know. He agrees that Dixie is in its final throes and contends that it will be possible to fix the exact moment of the demise. It will come, he says, when a rich Negro leaves behind a widow with sufficient holdings to justify one of the Snopes boys' marrying her for her money.

CHAPTER 8

FROM THE POTOMAC
TO EAGLE PASS

B Y ALL THE ordinary tests Texas must be counted
as Southern. Slave-owners opened up the eastern
reaches of the vast territory and promoted its
severance from Mexico; the state is still counted among
the major cotton producers; and it was one of the eleven
that departed the union after Fort Sumter. *The Yellow
Rose of Texas,* which recently inspired the Broadway
guitar pickers to new depths, was originally a bouncing
Confederate marching song, slightly altered by Sherman's
march to the sea which led the retreating boys in gray
to render the refrain: "And the gallant Hood of Texas
played hell in Tennessee!"

But, viewing the Lone Star state with the special snob-
bery of the eastern seaboard, Texas has never seemed
really Southern to me. Nothing happened to disabuse me
of that notion during the considerable period when I was
consigned by the Army to Austin and San Antonio. Nor

has it been altered in the years I have spent living next door, which, I might note, is rather a nervous business.

The reason, I suspect, is the vast distance from the Potomac to Eagle Pass. The impact of the Tidewater *mores* was greatly diminished by the time the Old South reached its farthest outpost in Texas. On the other hand, the frontier tradition, which helped shape the social patterns of the Southern interior, was nowhere stronger. There were cattle in Texas as well as cotton; cowboys as well as planters. A substantial portion of East Texas might have become a typical Southern state had it been carved off the mass and left to stand alone. But this was never done, and from the beginning there has been a special curl to the brim of the Texas hat, and a special twang in the Texas drawl. This was not solely a matter of terrain and economics; before and after the Civil War the explanation for the disappearance of a neighbor in the older sections of the South was commonly reduced to the shorthand G. T. T.—Gone To Texas—and it was, more often than not, the wild ones who went.

By the turn of the century Texas gave signs of settling down. There were then cotton and cattle barons who enjoyed the pretensions of third generation wealth, and they imposed a sense of order and propriety upon the older towns; nowhere east of Fort Worth was it necessary, or fashionable, to wear a six-gun on the hip or even a derringer in the sleeve. Then, in 1901, Spindletop blew in and oil made Texas a frontier all over again.

Elsewhere I have described the change in the ruling caste of the South as a gradual process of mutation. In

Texas a new guard sprang into being almost literally overnight; the first big oil strikes created a whole new class of millionaires, and major discoveries in the Twenties swelled the ranks. They were, in the nature of the oil business, gambling men; H. L. Hunt, who may be the richest man in the United States, was a professional poker dealer in South Arkansas when the wells came in at Smackover and set him on the way to a maharajah's annual income. If some of the others came of gentler backgrounds they nevertheless had to have the same steady nerves and disdain for caution if they were to sit in on a game in which all a man's money had to be on the table before he found out whe'ier ¹ · had drawn a full house or a busted flush.

The manner in w ᵤn che oil business is still conducted in Texas half a century after the first wildcatters became Big Rich brings goosebumps to more traditional financiers. The old-timers normally have a fine contempt for lawyers and bankers, with their fussy talk of contracts and collateral. They still make their fabulous deals by telephone or in what might appear to be casual conversation. And the system works in practice because the gambler's code has prevailed; a man's word is literally his bond, and if he reneges he's out of business. I sat bug-eyed in a New York hotel suite not long ago while a Texan I know wrapped up a pipeline deal involving upwards of fifty million dollars. My friend doesn't make as many headlines as some of his contemporaries, but he can still afford to take a hand in a friendly game at the Houston Petroleum Club. I had been asked by for a drink; when I arrived the bottles had been broken out, but they were being used to weight down the corners of maps spread over the floor. On their knees, my host and a new-found partner went over the maps, took a drink out of the neck of the bottle, shook hands, and thereby concluded an arrangement that involved some sort of involved stock swap, and, I gathered from their delighted chuckles, dealt Standard Oil a mighty blow.

All the new breed of Texas millionaires are not exclusively or even primarily oil men; there is, for instance, a mild-mannered fellow whose standard joke is the diffident explanation that he doesn't really own much property, a mere forty acres of land—in downtown Dallas. One of the most conspicuous, the late Jesse Jones, made his pile in banking, real estate, newspapers, and other enterprises which obviously did not suffer from his New Deal connections with the Reconstruction Finance Corporation. But it was the oil men who let loose a flood of new capital in Texas, and they have left their imprint everywhere on the booming economy. Giants, Edna Ferber has called them, and the term is not inexact; if they are sometimes wonderfully eccentric it must be conceded that they generally act as big as they think. Temperamentally they are a varied lot; but if they have one common characteristic it is contempt for a safe 6 per cent investment. They began with the big risk and big pay-off and they have found no reason to doubt either their luck or their vision. I suspect that this, as well as the traditional capacity of the state government for looking the other way when money is being made, accounts for the recent Texas insurance scandals; it is hard to imagine a Texan willing to tie up his own or anybody else's cash in government bonds or the shares of a prudent New England investment trust.

This free-wheeling fiscal approach, I believe, is far more significant than the more flamboyant personal traits of the Big Rich which have created the caricature now firmly imbedded in the contemporary American social scene. The money, after all, is still for the most part in the hands of the generation that made it. Despite its special local color I doubt that the spectacular behavior of some of the Texans is much different from that of the railroad tycoons who built their great mansions on Fifth Avenue in the Gilded Age, or the hog barons who established their Gold Coast in Chicago. Glenn McCarthy's weakness for chorus girls seems to be no more pronounced than Diamond Jim Brady's, and a private airplane is no more ostentatious a mark of wealth than a private railroad car. And, as in any society, those who turn up in the headlines are more likely to be atypical than typical; if Colonel D. Harold Byrd likes to lead the University of Texas band at football games, and has been known to invite an entire Cotton Bowl full of spectators out to the house for a little party, his compatriot H. L. Hunt is a virtual recluse; Howard Hughes is known primarily for his hot pursuit of movie queens on three continents, but the late Lee de Golyer stayed quietly at home in Dallas not only collecting rare first editions but reading them.

It is true, however, that the nature of the new Texas wealth has given its holders a special interest in politics.

The Big Rich share the normal distaste of the wealthy for taxes, but they have a far more urgent reason for seeking at least negative control of the political processes. The oil industry is regulated, primarily by state agencies which determine the amount and character of the production in each field. So is the increasingly profitable by-product, natural gas. But above and beyond all this there is the federal depletion allowance—the unique regulation which in effect puts a comparatively low tax ceiling on income derived from oil. The theory, which is sound enough, is that as they sell their oil the owners are in effect living off irreplaceable capital, and therefore receiving what amounts to a capital gain rather than a continuing income. The practice, which the Texans insist is equally sound, is that the oil producers retain a far greater proportion of their annual income than any other class of citizens in the republic.

These circumstances give the Big Rich an obvious stake in what goes on in Washington and Austin. In local politics they haven't had too much trouble. There they operate within the loose limits of the Democratic Party, which over the years has been splintered into factions which range all the way from New Deal liberal to America First conservative. No matter how the political wind veers, however, nobody has any reason to believe that the Texas Railroad Commission is likely to invoke any regulations adverse to the oil industry, if for no other reason than that the State of Texas itself is a large owner of oil property which produces public revenue in a quantity sufficient to keep state taxes reasonably low for all classes of taxpayers. So it is that the members of the Texas delegation to Congress may demonstrate a considerable disparity of views on matters removed from the Texas pocketbook but on oil they stand as one. Sam Rayburn is temperamentally the offspring of the old Southern agrarian revolt and is the acknowledged symbol of the regular Democrats. Lyndon Johnson, on the other hand, is one of the new breed of Southern politicians who keeps a cold eye on the main chance and has never been carried away by abstract notions of party loyalty. Nevertheless, the two display equal zeal in their guardianship of the oil interests —one in a key position as majority leader of the Senate and other as speaker of the House. And when Ralph Yarborough, who repeatedly ran for office under the banner of the New Deal, finally made it to the Senate, there was no reason to believe that this represented any shift in the voting balance as it affects oil and gas.

In national politics the Big Rich have, with only rare exceptions, openly thrown in with the Republicans in the last two elections—and Texas has gone heavily for Eisenhower. Some of them doubtless departed from the party of their fathers simply to hedge their bets; they figured they were in good shape in Congress, but with the constant pressure against the depletion allowance and the new drive for federal regulation of natural gas they thought it might be well to have an in with the White House. Indeed, in 1952 they made an open deal with Mr. Eisenhower. Governor Shivers, who obviously spoke their mind, paid a formal call upon Adlai Stevenson at Springfield and offered him Texas' electoral vote in return for a pledge to support the state's claim to the offshore oil lands. Stevenson declined, but Eisenhower accepted; and Shivers took the stump for the Republican ticket with the major Texas newspapers providing a solid claque for the new doctrine of Independent Democracy.

It would, however, be a mistake to attribute this new look in Texas politics solely to the self-interest of the Big Rich, and the vastly more numerous Little Rich who are enjoying unprecedented prosperity as a result of the flood of local investment capital. There is involved in it also a substantial element of chauvinistic political philosophy. When Texans brag that they can get along very well without the federal government, they come close to speaking the truth. The senators filibustering against the surrender of the federal government's rights to the tidelands considered making the debater's point that after all the United States did provide naval protection for the Texas Gulf coast; but they wisely decided against it on the sound ground that Texas undoubtedly would be delighted to build a navy of its own. The philosophical compound also includes the self-made man's usual contempt for social legislation; if I started broke and made 40 million dollars, the rationale goes, any man with git-up-and-go can at least make a living for his family without any help from the government.

The extreme manifestation of this sort of thinking has been displayed in the strange career of H. L. Hunt. The Dallas Croesus' concern was not with local politics, but with the nation's and the world's. In 1952 he turned up, a shadowy figure in the hotel corridors, at both major party conventions in Chicago, ready to make his pinto-choking bankroll available to the Republican and Democratic candidates of his choice. No man ever picked two longer shots—Douglas MacArthur and Richard B. Russell of Georgia—and this unhappy experience apparently convinced Hunt that the general public wasn't quite ready for his philosophy. He then concentrated on a massive grass-roots "educational" campaign through something he called Facts Forum, a public relations enterprise that broadcast right-wing propaganda nationally by direct mail and network radio and television. At one point Hunt wrote a model constitution, a document that would have reduced the powers of government below the level exercised by the original federation of American colonies, and reportedly shopped around for a Southern legislature that might be interested in adopting it as a pilot project for the nation. It is doubtful that Facts Forum, which now has been abandoned, accomplished much except to provide lucrative employment for a phalanx of publicists who periodically convinced their angel that the barricades would go up in the streets if he didn't reach for his checkbook. Hunt always seemed to me an innocent without any real understanding of the vast power that goes with vast wealth—a three-year-old waving a loaded revolver, dangerous, certainly, but not consciously vicious.

There are, however, more sophisticated types abroad on the Texas prairies, and they bring a sort of frontier ruthlessness to politics. In the current issue of race, for example, Texas has no real problem except in a relatively few eastern counties where Negroes are numerous and

Deep Southern *mores* are strong. In the wake of the 1954 Supreme Court decision Governor Shivers announced a policy of compliance, and the Texas state superintendent of education indicated that he saw no great dislocations ahead. But when Shivers ran into stiff competition for re-election from the liberal Ralph Yarborough, he didn't hesitate to ride the race issue for all it was worth—and it may have been worth his narrow margin of victory. The Big Rich, who have every reason to view Shivers with approbation, lent their support to an uninhibited propaganda campaign which equated the NAACP, the CIO, and the Communist Party. This sort of extremist talk, which is echoed in many of the newspapers, lends aid and comfort to perhaps the most active lunatic fringe now practicing in any major American city except Los Angeles —the Minute Women of Houston, who on the issue of textbook censorship finally succeeded in driving the long-suffering local superintendent of schools out of office.

All of this, however, seems to me not so much an alarming conspiracy as the natural product of the spirit of the posse. The Big Rich are as impatient of due process of law as they are of the conservatism of Eastern bankers; when someone gets in their way, they invoke Judge Roy Bean's law west of the Pecos: give the varmint a fair trial and then take him out and hang him. This is hard on the hapless souls who attempt to oppose the oil-powered juggernaut, but the same impatient drive produces remarkable results when it is turned to good purpose, as it frequently is. It may result from nothing more than chauvinistic devotion to the slogan, Everything's Big in Texas; but it is also true that the outward manifestations of culture are blossoming under the Lone Star along with the platinum mink coats and outsize Cadillacs. Major symphony orchestras are sawing away in Dallas and Houston, serious theatrical ventures are handsomely endowed, museums and libraries of stature are coming into being, baritones bend the bluebonnets with Wagner or Bach or anything else they choose, once they have rendered an introductory passage of *The Eyes of Texas*.

I would not say the Big Rich have yet had a comparably benign influence on education. A few years ago they ran off the president of the University of Texas because they regarded his economic and social views as unorthodox. (However, it should be noted that one of their own, Major Jubal Parten of the Woodley Petroleum Company, as chairman of the University board fought the ouster to the last.) But they are turning loose sums of endowment money for local institutions that could in time make many of them balance-sheet rivals of the Harvard Corporation. Sometimes this is no more than whimsical, as in the case of Hugh Roy Cullen, who once rewarded the University of Houston with a new building for winning a football game. Some of it is simple self-interest; a man in the oil business has an obvious stake in maintaining an ample supply of geologists. But much of the money goes without strings, and is reflected in genuine enrichment of institutions like Baylor, Rice, Southern Methodist, and Texas Christian.

It can be assumed that the passing of generations will have a gentling effect on the Big Rich, as it has had on the heirs of older American fortunes. Their sons and daughters have arrived at maturity in the long shadows of the outsize characters who sank the first wells, and they are not much heard of. But they undoubtedly will make some sort of mark of their own when they come into their heritage and some are anxious to get started; one has remarked desperately of his father, "If he can't take it with him, he's apparently not going." But the second generation is more likely to be distinguished by the narrow lapels of the Ivy League than by the broad brim of the Texas hat, and it is reasonable to presume that some of its members will display qualitative as well as quantitative interest in the fine arts. It is even possible that we may again see a hell-roaring political liberal with a Texas-size bank account—something that has been conspicuous by its absence since Maury Maverick joined the riders in the sky.

I have dealt at some length with Texas because it seems to me that the shape of the New South's future may be seen there. Texas is at least a length ahead of the other Southern states in the drive for economic parity with the nation, primarily because of the accident of oil. But the whole of the South is rapidly becoming a new economic frontier, and Texas-style wheeler-dealers are on the rise everywhere. Nobody has time for courtly conversation over a julep these days; it's bourbon-and-branch and let's get down to cases.

It's not that the Texans are staking out enclaves for themselves in the older Southern states; most of the Big Rich have enough to occupy them at home, and those who employ their dollars and their talents abroad are likely to move directly into the national financial arena where they can pick up baubles like railroads, publishing houses, and the like. But, just as the Tidewater gentry left its imprint on the Old South without joining the westward migration, so the Texas Big Rich serve as models for all the up-and-coming Southerners who figure there are fortunes to be made out of the currents of change flowing everywhere in the region.

There is every reason why the South's new business leadership should regard the Texans with awe and respect. The promoters in the older states consider the region's long-standing inferiority complex one of their greatest handicaps; they fervently preach the gospel that poverty does not result from an act of God, but can be cured by self-help. If Texas has a problem in this regard, it is a superiority complex; the extraverted ruling caste has convinced the citizenry that anything is possible, and so far have backed up the conviction with such concrete miracles as the Houston ship canal which converted that inland city into a major port. If this required a considerable measure of federal boondoggling, the Big Rich are never ones to let political philosophy stand in the way of practical gain; their representatives in Congress are capable of defending states' rights in a speech demanding more and better federal drought relief. Whatever they go after, the Texans never cast themselves as supplicants; they demand what they want as a matter of right.

Although Texas does not have so pressing a need for outside capital, the state still has done perhaps the region's most effective job of bringing in foreign corporations to share in and contribute to the new economic bonanza. It may be, as some of the neighboring states sometimes complain, a case of the rich getting richer. Even so, the Southern industrial promoters study and adopt the techniques of such public relations geniuses as the late Amon Carter of Fort Worth. Celebrities all over the world own white ten-gallon hats with sweatbands emblazoned in gold, A Friend of Amon Carter. And many an eastern tycoon has been bemused by a Fort Worth reception that included a ride to Carter's ranch in a refurbished Stanley Steamer, a tidal wave of rare bourbon poured from bottles that bore Carter's private brand, and a banquet that opened when the host called for attention by firing two six-guns into the air. It is, of course, true that those who in considerable number were persuaded to erect plants in Fort Worth were also offered more tangible inducements; but no one has been more effective in attracting attention to his city than the late proprietor of the *Star-Telegram*.

Increasingly the South's new business leadership displays a political affinity with the Texans. A generation ago the South's rich men, such as they were, were almost without exception yellow-dog Democrats. (The classic Southern test of party loyalty is the willingness to vote for a yellow dog if the Democrats nominate one.) If Franklin Roosevelt alarmed them by continuing his social experimentation after the edge of the depression had been blunted, Woodrow Wilson remained their ideal. The generation thus conditioned by its one-party heritage and the self-interest of a still predominantly agrarian economy is however now rapidly giving way to a business leadership that went over in considerable majority to the Republicans when General Eisenhower provided a convenient bridge. The new gentry still votes Democratic in local elections, primarily because there is rarely effective Republican competition; but their hearts and pocketbooks have been with the GOP in national contests. In the 1956 campaign I could detect no perceptible difference in the political patterns of the South's new suburbias and those in the nation at large; Independent Democracy, if not outright Republicanism, had become the stamp of respectability and virtually a requirement for membership in a proper Southern country club.

It may be, as the five hand-wringing Southern Republican Congressmen apparently believed when they went to President Eisenhower with a plea that he get the federal troops out of Little Rock in order to save the fledgling Southern wing of the Party, that the immediate prospect of building a two-party system in the South has been Faubused. Indeed, the shortrange result may well be a three-party system, since it is difficult to see how those who refuse to vote for a Republican because of Mr. Eisenhower's stand on Civil rights can vote for any Democrat who has a chance to be nominated in 1960. The bolt, if it comes, would probably wipe out the local Republican gains of recent years; but it would serve the GOP nationally just as well as a direct victory in Dixie, since its net effect would be to pull some Southern states out of the Democratic column and simply throw away their electoral votes. None of this, in any event, is likely to change the private views of the New Southern business leaders who, however they may classify themselves publicly, have become in fact and will likely continue to be political independents.

Like the Texans, these New Southern businessmen equate their own interests with the public's and attempt to shape local politics accordingly. There is nothing new in this, of course, but the industrial promotion campaigns have given the business community new leverage on the machinery of government. Its leaders now are able to oppose corporate and upper-bracket personal income taxes on the high ground that such levies would retard industrial growth and thereby keep the poorer classes from improving their incomes—and there is obvious merit in the contention, although it is equally obvious that the initial beneficiaries are those who already enjoy high corporate and personal incomes. On the other hand they, like the Texans, have also thrown their considerable weight behind more abstract causes. Public education in the South has received increasingly effective support from the industrial promotion campaigns. Better schools are a necessity, as the new factories demand personnel with higher technical skills; moreover, a good school system is a positive lure, and a bad one a positive deterrent to the executives who contemplate moving south to establish a new plant or a branch office. Legislatures which have long turned deaf ears to the pleas of professional educators are usually pushovers for the industrial promoters; the Arkansas Industrial Development Commission, for example, not only provided major assistance in passage of an additional one-cent sales tax for education, but almost without reference to the University of Arkansas persuaded the legislators to appropriate upwards of a half a million dollars for a new institute of technology.

Just as the Texans make a career of remembering the Alamo, so will the New Southerners, I suppose, continue to pay public homage to Marse Robert and the vanished glory; after all, it gives a special fillip to the public relations campaign. But their concern is with today, and their eyes are fixed on the future, not the past. Some aspects of their vision may be alarming; but there seems to me no doubt that the road they are looking down leads inevitably to reunion.

CHAPTER 9

THE NEW
KNOW-NOTHINGISM

IF I AM CORRECT in assuming that the handmaidens poverty and ignorance have been the great deterrents to material progress in the South, and the ultimate foes of human dignity, there is reason for a sanguine long-range view of the future. For the first time in history any Southerner who wants to work can now find a job that will at least leave a little cash money after the necessities are paid for. And for the first time practically all the South's children have access to twelve grades of schooling, and the schools are getting better. The means of refuting H. L. Mencken's charge that the South is the Sahara of the Bozart are finally at hand and, on the practical level at least, work is in progress.

Understanding of the South begins, however, with recognition of how short a time this has been true, and of how poor Southerners have been through most of the region's history—poor not only in comparison with more favored sections of the United States, but in terms of their own truncated ambition. There were cyclical fluctuations in the Southern economy from the Civil War to the First World War, but the peaks were never high enough to pull the mass of whites and blacks above the level of minimum subsistence. The roaring boom of the Twenties touched the South only briefly; the Great Depression came to the region early and stayed late. It is only in the last decade that Southerners have come to enjoy the unfamiliar feeling of relative financial security.

For all except the extraordinarily gifted, poverty of person breeds poverty of spirit. An illiterate may sing a charming ballad, but he can neither write a poem nor read after those who have. And ignorance makes a man peculiarly vulnerable to false fears and false hopes; native common sense provides no adequate defense against a dedicated fanatic or a wily charlatan who sets out to play upon the emotions of his fellows.

A substantial number of Southerners (but significantly never a majority until late years) have always managed to defeat the handmaidens. Some did it simply by dropping out through the bottom of organized society. There were both whites and Negroes in this class, men who recognized early in life that the odds were long against their earning an income sufficient to maintain the minimum trappings of respectability, and overwhelming against their attaining the good life through sweat of the brow. By conscious decision, then, they simply rejected the prevailing standards and proprieties and devoted their talents and their strength to their private pleasure and edification. They were to be found in the rural places and the small towns—great hunters and fishermen and usually great lovers, naturalists of considerable practical attainment, and detached students of human nature. They were a constant frustration to their more conventional fellow citizens; intelligent and able, they refused to work for money beyond the minimum required for tobacco and shells for their guns. And they were a source of unadmitted envy too, for they spurned all those ties to community or individual that halter a man and wither his youthful dreams. These naturals owned no house or barn or mule or marriage license, and aspired to none; they left their woods' colts cheerfully behind for someone else to raise when the time came, as it always did, to move on. It could not be said that they contributed nothing. The maidens who retired with them to the brush were left with memories that would lighten the drab years of domesticity; the small boys who followed them along the creeks and trails absorbed a sure knowledge of nature and a lifting feeling for the woods and fields; the loafers at the crossroads store who bothered to listen frequently heard the primitive wisdom of first-rate philosophers. In the nature of their vocation, however, they made no attempt to influence their time, and so they left no mark that could not readily be erased by the determined men who set out to order rural Southern society in their own image, and that of a fundamentalist God.

There was a considerable group at the other end of the scale, too, who rose above the norm and sought in books a broader view of human nature and of society. Learning and a decent respect for the classics were hallmarks of the original Southern gentry and all who aspired to their company. For many years formal schooling was beyond the reach of all except the prosperous and the poor who were equipped with an iron determination. But in time the drive for education became a spreading passion; many a man who had to sign his will with his mark resolved that his son would fare better, and held to his goal by dint of great sacrifice. From the time the old, scattered private academies began to give way to tax-supported schools near the end of the last century, each Southern generation, white and Negro alike, has been largely dedicated to the proposition that its children would be better educated than its own members were. The depth of that resolve may be seen in the fact that the South has long spent a higher percentage of its income on public education than any other region.

Still, with all that heart and effort, the schools the South could afford, outside the cities, were poor; the buildings were often primitive, the teachers ill-trained, the terms short. If the illiteracy rate declined year by year, it provided no measurement of deficiencies beyond the level of reading and writing; most rural children still had to drop out of school when they reached a height and weight that enabled them to work in the fields. This was the shrinking but dominant pattern until the middle-Thirties. In the remote mountain reaches of Madison County, Orval Faubus, now the 47-year-old governor of Arkansas and quite

possibly the inadvertent author of the final, shabby foot-
note to the great human tragedy that is the history of the
Old South, never attended school as long as six months in
a single year, and was himself a teacher in a one-room
school before he had completed the eighth grade.

In such an ambitious and largely unlettered society it
would seem that educated men would command respect,
and in a sense and for a time they did. I can remember
when the small Southern towns made a special dispensation for those whose professions attested a college degree
or at least an equivalent acquaintance with the printed
word—the doctor, the lawyer, the banker, the editor, the
teacher, and the preacher (although the casual practices
of ordainment among the Baptists robbed the last of cer-
tainty). They were considered a sort of informal court
which should be heard on large questions of public
policy, and they were even allowed a certain latitude in
personal behavior; an educated man might be caught
reading with his feet on his desk in the middle of the day
without being marked down as indolent, or he might sit
up late at night peering at the stars through a telescope
without being written off as a hopeless eccentric. The educated were granted status without the necessary requirement of wealth, and they were consulted.

This special identity has been lost with the rapid increase of the educated class in recent years; although the
percentage of graduates in the South still lags behind the
nation's, the college degree has become commonplace and
the institutions of higher learning reflect a steady upward
trend in enrollment. Few of the Southern colleges and

universities could be rated as distinguished, but they are good enough and numerous enough to make higher learning readily available everywhere in the region. The South, then, finally has a complete educational structure that provides universal exposure to at least a minimum of book learning.

Yet the region continues to be essentially hostile to the intellectual process—indeed, in the wake of the current racial tension, is perhaps more so than it has been in years. One of the least conspicuous but most significant manifestations of the Negro problem has been its generally stultifying effect upon free inquiry. The turning point came in the 1830's. Earlier Southern leaders, acting in the humanist tradition of Jefferson, had freely examined the peculiar institution of slavery, recognized its moral and economic defects, and openly discussed means of ameliorating them —including abandonment of the institution itself. Antislavery societies flourished in the region and men of standing participated in them. Abolitionist sentiments were expressed in respectable newspapers, and the movement reached a climax in the open debates on emancipation in the Virginia legislature in the session of 1831–32. "The institution was denounced as never before," Joseph Roberts wrote. "It was condemned wholesale fashion by the legal representatives of a slave-holding people. The vigor and breadth of the assault provided the debate with its most obvious distinction."

The proslavery element, of course, not only won the Virginia debate but quickly saw to it that no such heresy would sound again in the South. By 1837 there was not a single antislavery society left in the region, and social sanction was so complete that the subject of Abolition was literally almost never mentioned. Nor was mere silence enough; a Southerner was not permitted to simply retire from the field, he must join actively with the proslavery group if he were to avoid being suspect. C. Vann Woodward has described the genesis of the pattern:

Of the thousands of voices that had been raised in outspoken protest a short while before there were to be heard only a few whispers. Opponents changed their opinions or held their tongues. Loyalty to the South came to be defined in terms of conformity of thought regarding one of its institutions. Past records and associates were scrutinized closely, and the recency with which one had denounced Northern abolitionism became a matter of public concern. The South concentrated its energies upon the repression of heresy and raised intellectual barricades against the ideas of a critical and unfriendly world. The institution that had so recently been blamed for a multitude of the region's ills was now pictured as the secret of its superiority and the reason for its fancied perfection.

A century and a quarter later the pattern remains in full force and effect. The subject of integration in the public schools is off limits for Southern intellectuals; they discuss it only at their peril, and those subject to official reprisal or sensitive to social pressures have been made fully aware of the price they must pay. When the dean of the School of Education at the University of South Carolina, feeling a natural compulsion to speak out on a matter in his professional field, suggested that it might be possible to work out a plan for gradual abandonment of segregation, he was promptly drummed off the campus. A professor at Auburn met a similar fate when he wrote a letter on the subject to the student newspaper. Since many, and very probably most, Southern university professors consider the Supreme Court decision morally correct and accept some form and degree of integration in education as inevitable, it can be seen, as Professor Iredell Jenkins of the University of Alabama has written, that they face an urgent moral dilemma. Six Alabama professors who resigned in 1956 gave the Autherine Lucy incident as the reason. Professor Jenkins, in an article in the *Yale Review*, makes the point that the incident has also had a profound effect on many of those who remained. Finding themselves in personal opposition to the declared public policy of their state government, and feeling that they could and should contribute something to the resolution of the great social problem of their time, they face a choice between resigning or cultivating their gardens in the hope that the storm will soon blow over. The philosophy professor states the dilemma in these terms:

But it requires an extraordinary degree of intellectual certitude and moral assurance to publicly wash one's hands of a great university and assert that its case is hopeless, while it requires an arrogance which is either divine or demonic to adopt this attitude toward a whole huge section of the country. On the other hand, to prepare for a future that one may never see demands a patience and a faith that many do not possess.

While no great number of educators have been fired outright for voicing their racial views, or have formally resigned in protest against university policy, there is no doubt that the great intellectual blight has produced a steady and mounting drain on Southern faculties. It is not that many of the professors are by temperament action- ists or, in the Southern term, agitators. But, since the rela- tionship between the races is intertwined in virtually every aspect of Southern life, they run into the matter head on in any line of inquiry they may undertake out- side the pure sciences. Under stated or implied injunction to take no unpopular stand on the issue, or even to discuss it if it can be avoided, they are trapped by an ultimate professional frustration. They may never fling a resigna- tion on the president's desk or make any monument to the reason for their departure; but increasingly they pass word of their availability at the meetings of their profes- sional societies. And here too it is likely to be the most able or the most promising who accept the outside bid, men who have long had a standing opportunity to im- prove their personal fortunes but have accepted one of the generally lower Southern academic salaries out of a sense of dedication and identification with their native region. The president of a leading Ivy League college told me not long ago that he now has the choice of the top men on Southern faculties when he has a vacancy—a situ- ation, he noted, that had not prevailed for some years.

The professors provide only the most conspicuous ex- amples of the effect of the new Know Nothingism on all Southern intellectuals. Those whose professional activity brings them in constant contact with the issue—journal- ists, ministers, and to a lesser degree lawyers—feel the full force of pressure for conformity. In the Deep South they may be subject to an organized boycott by the Citizens Councils or the Klux, and there is at least the remote possibility of physical violence. And everywhere in the South the mildest public questioning of the sanctity of segregation brings some degree of condemnation and abuse. Today, as in the 1830's, even silence does not afford protection against the fanatics and their uninhibited party press; unless a man goes the whole way with fervid condemnation of the United States Supreme Court and all its works, he is subject to charges of disloyalty and heresy.

I do not suggest that the situation is intolerable, but it is obviously unpleasant. The tendency is for all except those of the deepest conviction to avoid the subject of race even in casual conversation. There is, I believe, a considerable mass of white Southerners in this position of unhappy, frustrated silence. Those who are of a religious bent must recognize, as the organized denominations have formally done, that a religion which exalts the brotherhood of man cannot consistently support a system which denies equal opportunity on the basis of race; not even the most determined bigot can make a segregationist out of the gentle Jew, Jesus Christ. Nor can a thoughtful man make the practice of legal segregation jibe with the basic tenets of American democracy. And finally, these Southerners recognize that as a practical matter the whole structure of law and order is gravely threatened by the defiance of the fanatics. Yet a man who voices these mild and reasoned sentiments even among his friends is likely to precipitate a social crisis; in almost any gathering there is likely to be one or more who will take violent exception and begin mouthing the old, bitter clichés.

The practical importance of this condition cannot, I think, be overemphasized. In the first place, it is quite clear that the process of transition from segregation to integration will raise many social problems of the first magnitude. Their resolution demands the talent and energy of the best minds in the South; nor is this solely a matter for the scholars, the intellectuals, and the advocates; it deserves the considered attention of practical men of affairs. Yet no such consideration is possible in an atmosphere in which the subject cannot safely be raised.

It has always seemed to me a remarkable and melancholy fact that I became an author in the field of race and education not by design, desire, or special interest, but by default. In 1954, when the Southern school cases were pending before the Supreme Court, the Fund for the Advancement of Education, upon the urgent recommendation of leading Southern educators, decided to finance a factual study of the region's dual school system. It was felt by the officers of the Fund, and clearly stated, that whether the Court ruled out legal segregation in public education or reaffirmed the *Plessy* separate but equal doctrine, the Southern public school system was in for a major overhaul. The great need was for objective information; it was a literal fact that there were not available even the basic data for measuring the physical disparity between white and Negro schools and thereby accurately computing the cost of equalization—whether this be done by merging the two systems or continuing them separately. Much had been written on the subject, it is true, but most of it was the product of advocates on one side or the other of the central moral issue and was colored by their views.

I have found no thoughtful person who has questioned the need for such a study. Yet the Fund quickly discovered that the subject was considered too hot for any Southern university to handle—this despite the fact that objectivity was the paramount consideration and the field of inquiry was one in which the universities themselves were obviously and intimately concerned. So in the end it was necessary to pull together a research staff of Southern scholars whose members signed up as individuals and not as representatives of the institutions that employed them, and to bring in a newspaper editor to head the undertaking. It also turned out to be impossible to bring together the presidents of the major Southern colleges and universities as an advisory committee to assist in determining the direction the project should take; all but a very few even declined to attend a private meeting to discuss the matter. We did manage to convene the chief state school officers to present for their final review the factual data we had gathered; but to do so we had to make an absolute pledge of no publicity and to agree that they would be given no published credit in the book, *The Negro and the Schools*, which was published coincidentally with the Court's ruling in May, 1954.

While I was occupied with the project I ran into an old politician who inquired what I was up to. I explained that

I was about to give birth to a book on Southern public education as it involved whites and Negroes. "Son," he said, "it sounds to me like you have got yourself in the position of a man running for son of a bitch without opposition." There have been occasions since when I have concluded that I have been elected by acclamation. Yet in that brief quiet time after the decision was rendered, the report was generally accepted in the South as an objective rendering of the facts in the case, and even praised as a useful contribution. My old friend Tom Waring of the *Charleston News and Courier* inspected it with the sharp and practiced eye of a working segregationist and declared that he could find no boobytraps. For a while I was in demand as a speaker on the subject before Southern audiences; but for some time now I have been largely ruled off the course. About the only invitations these days come from those wistful little human relations and church groups which bring together the dedicated moralists and the professional martyrs who see in the Negro's cause an opportunity to express their general rebellion against the community. It has worked the other way, too; Northern liberal groups have been offended by my insistence that segregation is going to continue as a practical matter until the mass of Negroes have improved their condition, for this violates a tenet of the counter-faith. In short I have become, in the wonderful lexicon of our muted time, a "controversial figure"—and I managed this not by fervently crusading for the downtrodden blacks, but simply by insisting that no Southern newspaper could possibly ignore the most pressing social issue its readers face, and that these matters must be fully reported and dispassionately discussed. It seems to me, indeed, that I have done no editorial battle at all; my rôle, rather, has been that of a man trying to preserve order at an incipient riot, and my highest purpose has been to see to it that calm and reasonable voices are heard above the clamor of the willful and ignorant men who have appropriated the center of the stage.

In the Upper South, of which Arkansas is a part, such a course demands no undue degree of courage, although a reasonably thick skin is useful. In the Deep South, of course, the hazards are greater. Yet even there, I am convinced, a man can survive without joining the stampede of the lemmings. Ralph McGill provides a case in point; in setting forth his views each day on the front page of the *Atlanta Constitution* McGill occupies a position of maximum exposure; he has himself described it as the eye of a permanent hurricane. But if he is the target of a spate of invective and the perennial object of the wrath of Georgia's ranking politicians, he is also a prophet not entirely without honor in his own country; the *Constitution* continues to flourish, and a recent readership survey showed that McGill's column is by long odds its most popular feature. Some of those who read it are bound to be impressed by McGill's counsel that, after all, Georgia is not going to secede from the union this time around, and in the end must achieve a rational and just accommodation for the state's Negro population. Editors of this stripe do not often carry the day on a specific issue; but the cumulative effect of their effort to keep a torch of reason alight is measurable. If McGill converts no single subscriber in a given edition, it is in large part the moderating influence of the *Constitution* over the years, I believe, that accounts for the fact that the citizens of Atlanta quietly re-elected Dr. Rufus Clement, a Negro, to the city school board in the same season that the wool-hat boys who control the legislature pushed through a resolution demanding the impeachment of the United States Supreme Court.

Most of the Southern newspapers have done a reasonably good job of accurately and fully reporting developments on the race front, and they deserve a measure of credit because they have done so in the face of sustained emotional pressures the like of which their contemporaries outside the region rarely encounter. Yet, like the politicians, the great majority of them have defaulted in their corollary role of leadership. Their proprietors generally have displayed symptoms of the illness that afflicts most of the nation's press: undue caution. Like their colleagues everywhere, Southern publishers are prone to stand in the bar of the country club and assume that they are listening to the voice of the people. The result is a steady watering down of the strength of their own position in the community; the loudmouths quickly discover that they will panic under the threat of pressure or even unpleasantness, and proceed accordingly. It is, sad to say, only the exceptions who recognize the elemental truth Jonathan Daniels of the *Raleigh News and Observer* once addressed to the American Society of Newspaper Editors—that basically journalism is not a respectable business, and the attempt to make it so inevitably perverts its purpose.

Bound by such strictures of policy, the working news-papermen of the South have done pretty well. Yet too many of these, too, have gone off on strange intellectual tangents that simply constitute an escape from reality. I have written elsewhere of the tendency to labor the states' rights doctrines of Calhoun as though they still had cur-rency a hundred years after the war that invalidated their basic premise. A more popular gambit is the You're An-other One school, of which Grover Cleveland Hall, Jr., of the *Montgomery Advertiser* is the acknowledged mas-ter. Hall occupies the editorial chair from which his father won a Pulitzer Prize in the Twenties for his successful campaign against the Ku Klux Klan. Perhaps the most eloquent editorial writer now practicing in the region, Hall presides over a page distinguished by a rare, wry wit; his caption for his comment on the end of Mont-gomery's long wearing controversy over bus segregation, for example, was a magnificent pun: "The Jig Is Up." Hall is too intellectually honest to contend that there is anything approximating equality of treatment for Negroes in Alabama, and he openly expresses his contempt for Alabama's White Citizens Councils. But his approach to the very real racial problems that beset his state largely consists of a running campaign intended to prove Negroes are even worse off in New York and Chicago. There is some merit in his contention, and by pressing it he infer-entially makes the point that if his subscribers are guilty of sin, it is not original. This may be soothing but it is irrelevant; the *Advertiser* circulates in Alabama, not in Harlem, and Alabama's problems, as Hall himself conceded when he deplored the fact that dynamite was being delivered to Montgomery front porches along with the morning paper, have now advanced far beyond simple questions of racial attitudes. When he gazes out of his office windows these days he looks upon a city in which it was recently demonstrated that it was not possible to assemble a jury that would convict white men of confessed violence against their Negro fellow citizens. Civilization, as Grover Hall fancies it, clearly cannot survive in such an atmosphere—and it seems to me that by fashioning his editorial page into a sort of moral escape hatch he is, whether he intends to or not, lending substantial aid and comfort to those Alabamians he acidly refers to as boobs and opportunists.

I doubt that there is going to be any peace for the Southern intellectuals for some time, and the indications are that the worst is yet to come. The organized propaganda campaign of the racists has been mounting for some time, and it has, of course, received an enormous boost from the default of Orval Faubus. In his press conferences and national television broadcasts the governor made several notable contributions to the arsenal of untruths, including the myth that the sternly-disciplined troops of the 101st Airborne Infantry were peeping toms who amused themselves by peering into the girls' dressing room at Central High School; this charge was proved a lie before the sun had set on it, but it will live on in the annals of the Citizens Councils. Most of the Southern states now have one or more publications of fairly wide circulation devoted to the destruction of any public man who dares to support the United States Supreme Court. Their editors are skilled character assassins, and, of course, they are for practical purposes beyond the reach of libel action. The South, which largely escaped the orgy of witch-hunting that took its name from the late Senator McCarthy, seems about to go off on an anti-Communist binge at the very moment the country is sobering up. It is now standard practice for the professional pamphleteers to equate integration and Communism; some of the old, shopworn professional witnesses of the McCarthy days have turned up before a Louisiana legislative investigating committee to read into the record long-discredited charges of Communist infiltration of human relations agencies and church groups which have been active in the field. For most of the racists, however, no such "evidence" is needed; they proceed directly to the conclusion that the South is beset by some sort of gigantic conspiracy, and since the current synonym for conspiratorial evil is Communism, they employ it for all it is worth.

The great frustration of the intellectual is that, bound by his own regard for facts and logic, he finds it impossible to debate with those who so viciously attack him. How, for example, does a man counter the wonderful reasoning of Eldon Lee Edwards, the imperial wizard of the Ku Klux Klan, who explains away factual information derogatory to his organization with the solemn statement that all the major Southern newspapers are under the control of the Anti-Defamation League and the NAACP? Blinking out from under the elongated silk dunce cap that is his badge of office, the wizard has gone on to tell a

national television audience that it is an established fact
that the NAACP is a Communist front organization. How
then, he was asked, does he account for the fact that
J. Edgar Hoover of the FBI has publicly pronounced the
NAACP free of any Communist taint, and has often
praised its work on behalf of individual rights as a major
contribution to the anti-Communist cause? Does the
wizard believe Hoover is an agent or a dupe of the Communists? Edwards has a complete and final answer. Of
course he doesn't consider Hoover pro-Communist. "But,"
he says firmly, "*if* J. Edgar Hoover really said that, he
didn't mean it."

A good deal of this nonsense, of course, falls of its own
weight. For one thing, any Southerner who is at all ob-
servant knows that the South traditionally has been a
desert so far as the Communist Party is concerned. While
the national Party leadership has always figured that the
real and fancied grievances of American Negroes should
make them a prime target for conversion, like so many
other Marxist theories this one has proved wholly faulty
in practice. A few frustrated Negro intellectuals and bemused Southern white sympathizers have joined the cause,
but it has never had any appeal for the colored mass,
which has an instinctive and healthy suspicion of the
hot-eyed zealot no matter what he is peddling. In more
than twenty years of the practice of journalism in the
South I can recall seeing exactly two known Communist
organizers at work even in the days when the Party oper-
ated above ground, and they were studies in futility. I

suppose there was some degree of undercover infiltration, but even if you take the excavations of the various Congressional investigating committees at face value, it is clear that the Communists never gained a tenable toehold in the region. Perhaps the most accurate test of the Party's strength in the South was the egg-spattered presidential campaign of Henry Wallace in 1948; it can be assumed that every Communist and sympathizer followed the Party line for Wallace, and that the confused messiah sucked along with them a fair number of innocents. In the eleven Confederate states, making the most extreme personal appeal for Negro support in history, Wallace polled 30,533 votes out of a total of 5,212,938 cast.

The racist propaganda line is distinguished not only by irrationality, but often by outright obscenity, and I doubt that any large percentage of white Southerners outside the certified lunatic fringe accepts it at face value. This is not, however, a matter of particular concern to its authors. The very wildness of the charges they hurl so freely serves their primary purpose, which is to intimidate any who may dare to dissent from the purest dogma of white supremacy. Too, it contains a calculated appeal to those who are prone to succumb to the human tendency to rationalize away any unpleasantness; white Southerners who fear the consequences of desegregation, and in some degree this includes the great majority, find an easy refuge in the reiterated notion that the highest court in the land is somehow illegal and without standing. It is a curious sight to see intelligent whites giving credence to spurious legalisms mouthed by shabby ambulance chasers they wouldn't employ to represent them in a five dollar debt claim in a justice of the peace court.

In this sense, then, the racists have been able to control the terms of the debate and distort it beyond the bounds of reason. But this condition cannot continue, for month by month each school district in the South moves closer to the time when the reality of the Supreme Court decision must be faced. As I have suggested, it is already possible to compute some of the cost factors—economic and social—in the present course of delay. The price of sustained defiance can be measured in terms of material progress, and ultimately it will have to be. And it can be measured, too, in the subtler but no less debilitating reduction in the quality of the Southern intellectual leadership; no people have ever prospered by exalting their fools and driving off their prophets. In any event, the final choice is as clear as it is hard: the South can maintain its public schools only by opening them to all its children without regard to race, thus leaving the continuation of the segregated pattern to genuinely voluntary choice. The only legal alternative is to close down the public school system entirely. This has been recognized from the beginning by every competent lawyer who has addressed himself to the subject; it is the basis of the private school programs authorized in most of the Southeastern states as a last resort. It was, significantly, the proposal Orval Faubus began talking up after it became clear that his peace-and-order gambit had failed, and that the only way he could keep his hand-tooled crisis alive was through the call for a special session of the legislature.

I don't know how white Southerners would behave if the default of responsible leadership permits the dead-end zealots to force this dread choice upon them. Before it happens, I hope, the muted voice of reason will be heard again, drawing the terms and stating the consequences as Jonathan Daniels did when he warned a South Carolina audience that ignorance is no defense against integration or anything else:

Nothing makes it a simple problem. But it can be made a more serious problem by those who step promptly, confidently, angrily forward with ruthless remedies. And the most tragic proposal ever made in a presumably intelligent land is that the South solve this great public problem by putting an end to public education—indeed to all education so far as the overwhelming majority of the people are concerned. The anger of those who propose such drastic remedies is understandable in the South, but what they propose should be understood, too, as something beyond secession from the Union. What they urge is secession from civilization.

CHAPTER 10

THE TERMS
OF PEACE

O N BALANCE I am, I think, an optimist. If I entertain serious doubts about the perfectibility of man, I cling to the belief that most of us are better than we usually have a chance to be. I don't know whether this is a universal truth or applies only to Southerners—we who are unique among Americans in that we have never shared fully in our country's great national success story. For the others the nation's history has been an unbroken succession of triumphs: the rolling back of the western frontier, the creation of a great and prosperous industrial society, the defeat of ranking world powers on land and sea, the spread of American influence around the globe. For us there was a lost war; we are the only Americans who have known defeat.

Arnold J. Toynbee, recalling Victorian England's Diamond Jubilee, wrote:

I remember the atmosphere. It was: well, here we are on the top of the world, and we have arrived at this peak to stay there—forever! There is, of course, a thing called history, but history is something unpleasant that happens to other people. We are comfortably outside all that. I am sure, if I had been a small boy in New York in 1897 I should have felt the same. Of course, if I had been a small boy in 1897 in the Southern part of the United States, I should not have felt the same; I should then have known from my parents that history had happened to my people in my part of the world.

Almost a hundred years have elapsed since Southerners could indulge in a comparable dream. Robert Barnwell Rhett spun a mighty vision in his speech on the occasion of South Carolina's secession, predicting that a historian in 2000 A. D. would write of the Confederate States of America: "And extending their empire across this continent to the Pacific, and down through Mexico to the other side of the great gulf, and over the isles of the sea, they established an empire and wrought out a civilization that has never been equalled or surpassed—a civilization teeming with orators, poets, philosophers, statesmen and historians equal to those of Greece and Rome. . . ." But the glory that was Dixie lasted less than five years.

Those who win a war can afford to forget it; those who lose apparently can't. Most Americans now think of the Civil War as ancient history; a majority come of families that had not even reached these shores when it was fought, and Second Manassas and The Wilderness must seem as remote from their daily lives as Thermopylae. Yet even Southerners who were not disposed to nurture the legends of the Lost Cause could not escape it. For one

thing, the War and its aftermath cost the South a generation as time is normally reckoned; until well into this
century privation forced many to marry late. My Yankee
contemporaries are usually surprised to learn that it was
my grandfathers, not my great-grandfathers, who served
in the Confederate Army. Their widows lived on into my
boyhood and regaled me with their memories while I
played with the cap and ball pistol issued to Pvt. William
Ashmore when he mustered into Hampton's Legion.

I could no more have escaped the past in the South
Carolina of my time than I could have given up breath-
ing. It was, first of all, a common topic of family conversation—not the details of a given Civil War battle, but the
matter of who a man was and whom he was kin to, and
why. The Ashmores made up a clan distinguished primarily by their number and the length of their residence
in Greenville County. The founders had come with the
first wave of Scotch-Irish, and the tombstones in the family burying grounds showed they had arrived before the
Revolution. Their migration was halted by the barrier of
the Appalachians, into which the county thrusts at the
apex of the South Carolina triangle. Marrying into the
other early-settling families, they bred so copiously they
soon constituted something approximating a local political
party. One of their own was in Congress by the time of
the Secession, and, reflecting the views of his yeoman
constituents, he was the only member of the delegation
who took the stump to speak against severing the union.
Eighty years later when I was sent as a young reporter

to cover the County Courthouse, it was something like attending a family reunion; Cousin John was the county supervisor, Cousin Robert the prosecuting attorney, and Cousin Maurice the tax collector. I once asked John, the political patriarch who had an obvious practical interest in genealogy, just whom I could honestly count as relatives. "Son," he said, "the way I figure it we're kin to everybody in this county, white or black, one way or another."

I grew up, then, in a place my own people, for better or worse, had helped create; if we actually owned very little of it (there were Ashmores of varying kind and condition, but I never met a rich one) it was nevertheless in a larger sense mine. And the mark of the clan was ineradicably upon me. There is sentiment in this, I know, and perhaps sentimentality, but I have never been entirely comfortable in any place where I cannot look out and see hills lifting into blue mountains.

When Buck Duke harnessed the upland rivers and made the cotton mills possible, our town became South Carolina's second city, and our county the state's most populous. So still more of us left the land, but we never severed all our ties; on the summer afternoons we would drive down to Possum Kingdom to visit the kinfolks, and when the cousins on the farm outgrew the country schools they came to live with us while they finished their studies. Funerals brought us all out. There was mourning, of course, when one of the clan was laid out at the Brushy Creek Baptist Church or the Presbyterian chapel at Lickville; but there was a spirit of reunion too as the women fanned and chattered under the chinaberry trees and the men slipped off to the spring for a nip at the forbidden jug.

I don't suppose this sense of identity with time, place, and the past was unique to Southerners; it existed certainly in New England and the older sections of the Middle-West. But circumstance gave it special force in the South, and it lasted longer. The growth of the cities and the accompanying shift to urban values came much later in the region, and we were, I think, somehow more reluctant to pull up roots grown so deep. My father, who left the farm in his early youth and enjoyed modest success as a merchant, never seemed entirely comfortable in his prim city clothes. As long as he could he kept title to a patch of red earth somewhere in sight of the mountains, and when the depression bankrupted him he went back like a wounded animal to make his last stand on the soil.

My generation is the first to have these roots severed entirely by the sharp edge of change. Some of us still live on the land, of course, and make a living from it; but today's farmer has the manner and the accoutrements of the corporation executive. He spends as much time bending over a hot telephone as he does walking his fields; he is a constant commuter to the cities now only minutes away; and the old homeplace has been remodeled to meet the latest requirements of *House and Garden*. Even the conscious rebels get no more for their pains than fresh air. My brother, weary of the New York canyons and finding Atlanta too much of a city, has gone back to the mountains of our youth. The wind still sighs through the pine trees there at Tryon, just over the Greenville County line, but it is likely to be drowned out by the rattle of cocktail crockery from the patios of his neighbors, all of whom seem to be retired Chicago stove manufacturers. And his financial umbilical cord still stretches back to the publishing house in New York.

You can't go home again, said Thomas Wolfe, who lived just over the ridge before the lonely echo of train whistles in the mountain valleys lured him forth to the web and the rock of Manhattan. And this is true because home no longer exists. Nor is this solely a matter of physical change, of a filling station that stands where an old house settled under the trees, or the sun glinting on miles of picture windows in the fields where a boy once followed his dog. Home was a matter of time as well as of place, of values trapped in amber.

In the 1920's there was a staunch effort by a little group of Southern intellectuals to rally the South and stem the tide. Centering around Vanderbilt University, they called themselves Agrarians, and in 1930 they produced a proud manifesto, *I'll Take My Stand*. There were distinguished names among those who contributed to the symposium—John Crowe Ransom, Donald Davidson, Allen Tate, and Robert Penn Warren. They cried out in protest against the materialism of the age and condemned the Southern liberals, from Henry Grady forward, for surrendering to it. We should not emulate the faceless Yankee and measure our worth in dollars and creature comforts, they insisted, but should hoist high the old standards. If a good many of us starved, and those with darker skins suffered injustice, we would still retain our freedom to nurture our God-given Individualism and seek, each in his own way, the paths of glory. Davidson wrote: "One ought to be able to say of [the South] as 'A. E.' said of Ireland, that it is a good field for the arts, especially for poetry, simply because, in contrast to progressive America, it has long been defeated and poor and behind the times; or, furthermore, because it offers its people belief rather than doubt, conviction rather than skepticism, loyalty rather than distrust."

This was intellectualism giving voice to the old concept of aristocracy, but much too long after the fact. Of the sixteen members who launched the little magazine, *The Fugitive*, in 1922, only four were left when the Agrarians took their stand eight years later; the others had become bankers, insurance executives, and the like, or scholars far removed from the field. The amber was shattered, the old values naked and exposed to the winds of change; the nation was no longer willing to let us be different, and in truth very few of us really wanted to be.

So it is gone now, whatever it was we had, and it doesn't really matter whether it was taken from us or whether we bartered it away. Not long ago I sat beside a wise and beautiful lady in a taxi on New York's East River Drive, alternately crawling and bowling toward that sweep of midtown towers which is surely one of the most astonishing examples of man's creative capacity, and of man's inhumanity to man. The sight, I told her, no longer disturbed me; I was, finally, at peace with New York. She, who had lived all her life around the metropolitan complex and had founded a family in the canyons while pursuing a successful professional career, was amused and curious. Did I mean that I had once considered myself at war with the city, and had felt a compulsion to conquer the capital of the arts? She had thought that sort of thing had gone out with Sinclair Lewis, that nobody since Carol Kennicott had felt it necessary to flee Main Street to pursue either the muse or Mammon. I agreed that this was largely so, but it was not, as so many thought, because there was really a new regional consciousness and a literary concern with the length and breadth of a broad land; rather it was that New York no longer had any boundaries, that it was everywhere that telephones and radio and television and airplanes could reach—for New York is not simply an uncomfortable place to live and work in, but a state of mind, and in that sense there is nothing left now to confine it, no physical barriers and no permanent, distinctive regional attitudes. So, I told her, I was at peace with New York not because I had conquered it, or tried to, but because I had surrendered; like my grandfathers I had turned in my sword because the invasion was complete and I had nothing left to defend.

So it will be seen that I, like my more sentimental contemporaries, read the South's history as something of a personal tragedy. But it seems to me that the tragedy lies not in the battles we lost, but in the battles we never fought. In 1951, that last year of Democratic primacy, I addressed myself to the point before the Southern Governors Conference at Hot Springs—the last time, I think, that the general subject of race relations has been on the agenda at a conclave of the public officials most immediately concerned with it. If, rereading my remarks these two national elections later, I do not find that what I had to say was particularly original, it does perhaps entitle me to a license as a prophet, junior grade. Suggesting that the very real race problem in the South was no more likely to yield to "impassioned denunciation of our outside critics, fancy political maneuvering, or partisan secession than it did to armed rebellion," I went on to urge the gentlemen there assembled to review the nature of the Southern dilemma:

The practical problem before the South is to preserve social segregation while at the same time meeting the conditions of a Constitution and a national tradition which demand that full civil liberties and full equality of opportunity be extended to all citizens without discrimination. If I read the election returns correctly, a considerable majority of the people of the United States have come to believe that this cannot be done, and therefore to support, or at least accept, a federal program of legislation that is clearly aimed at the immediate end of segregation. . . .

So far we have attempted to meet the constant assault on segregation largely by negative means. We have fought back, sometimes successfully, but our weapons have been those of an embattled political minority and they are poor things at best. Some of us have suffered under the delusion that the South is the victim of an evil conspiracy, and that if we could only remove a few key men from power our troubles would be over. This is nonsense, and it can be very dangerous nonsense. For every genuine radical or cynical political opportunist who exploits the race question for his own ends, there are ten thousand sober, sincere, essentially conservative Americans who have accepted the proposition set forth in the civil rights program proposed by President Truman and embodied in the platform of the Republican Party.

And the more we strike back in blind reaction to their demands, the more convinced they become that we are all misbegotten racists who will respond to nothing less than federal coercion.

Still in my prophet's robes, I suggested that while we in the South still controlled the situation we should chart a positive course:

We must recognize, first of all, that in fundamentally public activities—and the test here would be their support by tax funds—the Negro must either be treated without official prejudice or in absolute incontrovertible fact be provided with separate but equal facilities. When we have done this we can argue, and I think be heard sympathetically, that we have met the stated commitments of citizenship, and we may then insist that matters involved in the private relationship between the two races are, and should be, beyond the reach of law.

Certainly no one could have contended that these mild remarks were inflammatory, and no one did. But the march of events since 1951 seems to indicate that my audience also did not consider them relevant. James F. Byrnes, returned from Olympus to the governorship of South Carolina, must have then been well along with the plot to lead the South directly into the Republican fold. Fielding Wright of Mississippi, still bearing the scars of the Dixiecrat campaign of 1948, was perhaps entitled to a degree of umbrage. Herman Talmadge of Georgia listened with the polite silence of the closed mind. Only Theodore McKeldin, Republican of Maryland, responded with what appeared to be genuine enthusiasm—and this only depressed me, since I have never been willing to concede turncoat Maryland's claim to a Southern accent.

So the governors went forth to help pull down their own temple—refusing to face the problem they themselves counted as paramount, and worse still, trying to convince the world that it didn't exist. In 1952 and again in 1956 their intransigence—and in some cases their outright betrayal—disarmed their own party and armed their political enemy. This has made it possible for the Republicans, under the canny guidance of Attorney General Brownell, to fashion the civil rights issue into a sharp and deadly political weapon. With no present political stake in the region, and no historic sympathy for it, the Republicans have everything to gain and nothing to lose by insisting that there must be a sort of New Reconstruction. There is no evidence that the Eisenhower administration is genuinely concerned with the lot of the Negro—none, certainly, in the record of the President's flaccid inaction in the quiet time after the Supreme Court decision when the moral weight of his office might well have headed off the polarization of public opinion. I am inclined to agree with Doris Fleeson's verdict: "The Republicans make no distinction as to race; they simply don't care about people." But the Republican motive is irrelevant. The important thing is that the Republican position is fixed and it will not change—and it is no different in practice from that of the national Democratic Party. And the great irony is that both were irrevocably shaped by the South—by inaction in the days of grace, and by blind defiance when time began to run out.

Well, the skies will not fall—but they will arch over a different land when the transition is complete. Not changed, as Southerners fear, by widespread commingling of the races; on the contrary, one of the great losses may be that whites and Negroes will never again really know each other. There was a time, despite the violence and the idiocy, when whites and blacks in the South were neighbors in the best sense—ready to help in time of trouble, to comfort in time of sorrow. We are fated to be strangers now, as men are who live in cities and reckon their social problems in terms of mass movements.

And it was the knowing, I think, that was important and in the quieter time did much to take the curse off the system. Once we could consider our neighbors, white or black, one at a time; we could hate them as individuals, or love them, respect their strength and recognize their weaknesses, and forgive them if we saw fit. It was this pattern that held the promise of a way out, the promise the South acted upon for more than thirty years in a strangely neglected period of the region's history. Once they had restored order in the First Reconstruction, the South's only heroes—the old Confederates—proceeded on the assumption that the freed slaves would be citizens with full rights and privileges. General Hampton told Sir George Campbell, "The better class of whites certainly want to conserve the Negro." In Columbia Sir George saw for himself what this meant in practice and remarked that "the humblest black rides with the proudest white on terms of perfect equality, and without the smallest symptom of malice or dislike on either side. I was, I confess surprised to see how completely this is the case; even an English Radical was a little taken aback at first." And *The Richmond Dispatch*, today calling for interposition to preserve Jim Crow at any cost, in 1886 could proudly state:

Our State Constitution requires all State officers in their oath of office to declare that they "recognize and accept the civil and political equality of all men." We repeat that nobody here objects to sitting in political conventions with Negroes. Nobody here objects to serving on juries with Negroes. No lawyer objects to practicing law in court where Negro lawyers practice. . . . Colored men are allowed to introduce bills into the Virginia Legislature; and in both branches of this body Negroes are allowed to sit, as they have a right to sit.

When the South, reacting in part to the excesses of the contest between Populists and Bourbons for the Negro vote, laid in place the rigid barriers of legal segregation, the Negro lost much in terms of achieved advances and in hope for the future. But white Southerners lost too, and so did the nation, for the South had important things to say to Americans, and now no one would listen—and we ourselves would not be able to find words for the truths we knew and felt, not while we were occupied with such monumental irrelevancies as where a man should sit on a street car.

As members of a political minority in a democratic republic, Southerners of necessity had learned much about the nature of popular government. We knew, out of an experience shared by no other Americans, the weakness of pure democracy. Elsewhere in the nation the will of the majority had, without conspicuous exception, pushed the institutions of government in directions that best served the common good. In the South this was not always the case. Had secession, for example, been submitted to a plebiscite in the Southern states, it would have carried overwhelmingly—for there was no one of consequence to speak against it. When the South, after its promising start toward a resolution of the race problem after the Civil War, relapsed into dead-end racism it was not because evil men charted that course, but because good men grew weary and allowed uninformed popular opinion to have its way. So it is today; put the issue of desegregation in public education to a popular test in the Confederate states, with every Negro voting without restraint, and a negative vote is a foregone conclusion. The majority in the nation says legal segregation is wrong, the majority in the South says legal segregation is right—and it will take more than a simple tallying of votes to settle the issue here drawn.

Southerners can understand what the founding fathers were about when they set up a delicate system of balanced powers, making the legislative branch of government directly responsive to popular pressures, the executive removed to some degree, and the judiciary, in theory at least, largely immune. What the founders recognized, and too many modern Americans overlook in the tendency toward literal reading of freedom and equality, is that while the popular will is an effective check on tyranny, there also needs to be an effective check on the popular will—for tyranny is not the only, and perhaps not even the most important hazard of modern man. The South had reason to know exactly what Joseph Pulitzer was talking about when he equated the threat of the predatory poor, who are numerous, with that of the predatory rich, who are few.

The South insisted historically that another balance was as essential as that among the branches of the federal structure, the division of powers between the states and the central government. Calhoun saw this as a necessary brake on the popular will—not to finally nullify it, but to slow it until there was a concurrent majority, one, that is, in which the minority, while still opposing the majority view, is willing to accept it. The Civil War which did so much to discredit the Calhoun doctrine in a limited sense also vindicated it; when the Southern minority could not be brought to concur with the prevailing national view on slavery and the tariff, the union was sundered.

What the South was defending over the years, then, was the right to be wrong—wrong, at least, as a substantial national majority judged the issues of slavery and segregation. It is, of course, a basic right, the one upon which an entire structure of law has been erected to protect minorities. But the South debased it by using it as a cloak behind which the local Southern white majority denied the common rights and immunities of citizenship to the black minority. It was never enough to say simply that a majority wanted it that way and that their will, therefore, should prevail; it was clearly the duty of those who knew better to insist that the majority must recognize that the coin minted by Calhoun had two faces—that a system which might be temporarily tolerable and even necessary would become intolerable unless it evolved with the changing times. To insist otherwise, to say that come what may the Southern white minority would never concur with the national majority—as impassioned men are still saying —is simply to reduce the right of dissent to the right of revolution.

The South had reason to know, too, that there was still a third essential balance involved—and this beyond the mechanics of government. Rank, in the old army phrase, has its privileges; but each privilege is matched by responsibility. This was the essence of the original Southern concept of aristocracy; under it a man could respect the popular will without automatically bowing to it; believing it wrong it was his clear duty to try to change it. While this concept prevailed the South was able to field a magnificent army to fight a war it could not, and should not, have won. It was also able to accept its defeat with the grace enjoined by Robert E. Lee and begin in good conscience to make decent and honorable provision for the Negro slaves who were now to become citizens. When the concept began to fade, finally to survive only in the fussy preoccupation of the pompous with genealogy and manners, the South took its fatal turning.

It may be, as scholars have argued from de Tocqueville forward, that the American system could never provide the conditions necessary for the maintenance of an authentic aristocracy, that the equalitarian strictures against special privilege would in the end militate against the matching special responsibility. And it may be too that while the Southern experience has been unique, the larger issues raised by it are not. There is reason to wonder, certainly, whether the American system as it has evolved under the impact of the expanding cities is anywhere giving us the kind of public and private leadership our age demands—whether the focus has not shifted from boldness and vision to the comfortable common denominator.

In any event, and for better or worse, the South must now find its future in the national pattern. The angry cries of defiance sounding across the region do not echo a gallant past, only a contemporary temper tantrum. I have at hand a letter to the editor of the *Arkansas Gazette* which begins by dismissing all those who insist that the rulings of the United States Supreme Court are the law of the land as "pseudo-liberals, pinkos, Communists, dupes, and morons." And the impassioned bookkeeper who wrote it continues:

Harry Ashmore might refresh himself on the Second Amendment of our United States Constitution which says in part "the right of the people to keep and bear arms shall not be infringed." If reason and ballots do not avail us in the end, that amendment tells us what to do as a last resort. That amendment talks Anglo-Saxon. Cowardly people can't understand it.

Well, I have so refreshed myself. But when I look out the window of my editorial office, I gaze upon the bland stone façade of the local branch of the Federal Reserve Bank of St. Louis. And down the street I see the shining window that bears the sign Merrill Lynch, Pierce, Fenner & Beane. I can imagine many ceremonies taking place on the intervening stretch of asphalt—including a third-term inaugural parade for Orval E. Faubus—but not my fellow townsmen lining up in double rank while the chairman of the local White Citizens Council checks their bandoliers in preparation for a second march to turn back the Federals at Pea Ridge.

No, history does not run backward, and it buries its own dead. I can only hope that in the new time the triumph of the thin-lipped men is not absolute—that somehow we in the South can carry over traces of the old qualities of humor and grace that once distinguished most of us, proud or humble, black or white. If so, Dixie's epitaph can read simply: R. I. P.